A History of JUDO

柔
道
史

A signed portrait of Jigoro Kano, the genius who invented judo

A History of JUDO

Syd Hoare
8th Dan

Yamagi Books

First published 2009 by Yamagi Books

Address: Yamagi Books at PO Box 62765
London SW12 2AD

Website – www.sydhoare.com
Email info@sydhoare.com

British Library Cataloguing in Publication Data
A catalogue record for this book is available from the British Library
Hoare Syd
A History of Judo

ISBN-13 978-0-9560498-0-3

Acknowledgements
Bath University Library for Oxford University v. Police image
Kano Society for frontispiece portrait of Kano
Trustees of the British Museum for cover images

Yamagi Books acknowledges the use of the inset images which are taken from *Judo Kyohon*
by Kano Jigoro published in 1931 by Sanseido, from *Judo Kyohan* by Yokoyama and Oshima
published in 1924 by Nishodo and from *Judo Gojunen* by Oimatsu Shinichi published in
1955 by Jiji Tsushinsha. Every effort has been made to contact all copyright holders. Yamagi
Books will be grateful of any notification of additions that should be incorporated in the
next edition of this volume.

Also many thanks to eldest daughter Sasha who edited this book.

Designed by Bet Ayer, www.musicanddesignsolutions.com
Printed in Finland by WS Bookwell

Acknowledgements

From the time when I first started judo in London in 1954 as a keen fourteen year old I have been influenced by so many judoka both Japanese and non-Japanese that I hesitate to start listing them here. As far as writing goes the biggest influence was Trevor Leggett 6th Dan who urged us to sharpen our English and write about judo and not leave it to others. However I owe a large debt to the Kodokan where I trained in the 1960s. I regard this book as an *Ongaeshi* which is Japanese for 'repayment of a favour'. Although I have touched on some delicate matters in this history, the story of judo and Kano Jigoro towers above them all.

Syd Hoare

Other titles by Syd Hoare:

A–Z of Judo
Judo Strategies
Teach Yourself Judo
Teach Yourself Self Defence
Teach Yourself Keep Fit
Osoto-gari
Japanese Fighting Arts (Judo)
Know the Game - Judo

Contents

Ford

In 2005 I was asked to give five lectures on judo at Bath University as part of its European Judo Union Foundation degree course in Judo. I had a free hand and chose the history of judo and the history of the competition rules, in addition to some technical lectures. This plunged me into quite a lot of work and many pages of translation from Japanese sources as it became obvious that there was not much in English on the subject other than the obligatory page of standard history that prefaces most judo books. Articles on the internet provided some information but it soon became clear that often they varied from Japanese material that I had. In 2006 and 2007 I repeated the lectures to new students. However, I worked on them over that period and made several corrections and clarifications. As new facts emerged I came to the conclusion that the original story of judo would make a very interesting book and possibly assist the future development of judo. It was startling to realise how after one hundred and twenty six years from the founding of judo how little is known outside Japan about early judo and Kano Jigoro – the genius who invented judo.

Judo officially started in 1882 when Kano Jigoro set up a small dojo (training hall) in a Jodo Buddhist temple called Eisho-ji in Tokyo. He called his dojo the Kodokan (literally. Expounding the Way Hall) and described what he did there as Kodokan judo. However, the story of judo began very much earlier than that. Judo was partially based on jujitsu which in turn was based on other martial arts including kumi-uchi and sumo which stretched way back into the mists of Japanese time – before recorded history[1]. Kano's small dojo grew into a huge national organisation in Japan and subsequently judo became an Olympic sport in 1964.

[1] Jujitsu is a single Japanese word written with two characters. In English it can be written jiu-jitsu, ju-jitsu or jujutsu. The hyphen is not necessary. They are all pronounced the same. Jujitsu is perhaps best translated as Japanese unarmed combat systems of which there were many.

The first seventy years of Kodokan judo's existence, from its start in 1882 to the mid 1950s when international judo began to grow, was almost solely in Japan. Inevitably most of the history in this book is about judo in Japan although key international developments from 1950 are included (Judo's organisational development from the first world championships of 1956 would possibly make a second volume). During this long period judo encountered many problems and various attempts were made to rectify them. Judo still has unresolved problems such as the balance between standing work (throws) and groundwork (restraints and submission techniques). It is useful to know about Japan's past experience especially when trying 'new' solutions for these old problems.

The key figure in this history is Kano Jigoro[2], the man who created Judo. In my Japanese *Who's Who* he is described as an educationalist of the Meiji and Taisho periods (1868-1925) and the man who started judo. Education and judo were equally important to him. In contrast to the founders of other Japanese martial arts Kano was also an educational bureaucrat whose intelligence, organisational ability and foresight helped develop and guide his judo through some very difficult times in Japan.

The world has become familiar with the word judo but in many respects it remains a puzzle and is often confused with the other barefooted oriental martial arts which also wear white suits and denote grade by coloured belts. Judo is:

1. From a very successful oriental culture (second largest economy in the world)
2. Its principles, philosophy, etiquette and terminology are oriental.
3. Its roots go back many centuries making it one of the oldest 'sports' in the world
4. Practitioners are told they should do it for improvement in combat skills, physical fitness and moral strength
5. It is done in bare feet wearing a loose truncated kimono and grade and ability are indicated by a coloured belt worn around the middle
6. It is one of the grappling type martial arts which though not as spectacular as the striking martial arts such as karate is very effective in combat

[2] Kano is the family name, which comes first in Japan.

And yet judo is technically and tactically very complex with four distinct ways of winning with over one hundred throws not to mention its many restraints, strangles and jointlocks. It is physiologically and psychologically hard and bruising and it takes a long time to get good at it. So how did it become an Olympic sport?

All of the credit for this goes back to the founder of judo Kano Jigoro. Under a different founder judo might possibly have been only a footnote to a little-known subject called jujitsu. If Kano had not devoted so much time to judo in all likelihood he might have become minister of education in Japan or indeed prime minister at a crucial point in Japan's history. He was a man of phenomenal energy, intelligence and curiosity.

I have had to rely on the Japanese written record and in doing so chose what seems to be the most accurate, unbiased and authoritative account especially Professor Oimatsu's *Judo Gojunen*, 1955. History, it is said, is written by the victors, so in order to approach judo from different perspectives I have also referred to Japanese books on Budo, jujitsu, and other martial arts books including kendo and sumo, and books on Japanese history (see the Bibliography). History in the East is often 'airbrushed' and sensitive issues are avoided. There is the accepted version of events and there is the real version. In this history I have tried to be as objective as possible but I occasionally have the suspicion that things are not quite what they seem. I am sure that there is much much more to be discovered about Kano and judo and of course new material can turn conventional history on its head.

In this book I refer frequently to what Kano said or wrote but I do not always give a reference. To do this would litter the book with footnotes. Apart from the actual translations of original texts much of the book is inevitably my Western commentary and interpretation for which I take full responsibility. Luckily in this technological age books can be easily revised and updated so new original information will always be gratefully received.

Syd Hoare, London 2008

Chapter 1
From Ancient Sumo to Medieval Jujitsu

Kodokan Judo which was founded by Kano Jigoro in 1882 did not spontaneously combust. It was based on jujitsu which dates back to about 1530. However jujitsu was based on even older combat arts – kumi-uchi and sumo – that go back centuries to the point where real history merges into myth. Where did it all begin?

The creation myths

The earliest creation myths of Japan are to be found in two books. One is called the *Kojiki* and the other is the *Nihon Shoki*. Collectively they are known as the Kiki myths. They were compiled to list the genealogies and establish the credentials of the long line of Japanese emperors, from Jimmu (the first one enthroned in 660BC) and to record ancient myths, legends and traditional tales. The *Kojiki* was finished in AD 712 and the *Nihon Shoki* in AD 720. In a section entitled Age of the Gods are the old myths and legends, many of which cannot be verified by archaeology or other records. However, historically verifiable myths, legends and tales can be identified from about the 5th century AD.

In the Kojiki there is one myth about two gods, Takeminakata and Takemikazuchi, who fought for control of a province in Japan with a trial of strength (*chikara kurabe*). In the second book is a similar tale of two warriors, Kuehaya and Sukune, who are pitted against each other by Emperor Suinin. In the first fight Takemikazuchi wins with a throw and in the second the warriors fight and in an exchange of kicks Sukune breaks Kuehaya's ribs and then tramples him to death. These trials or comparisons of strength, known as chikara kurabe, are generally reckoned to be the earliest recorded sumo bouts although there is little in these two accounts that is similar to modern sumo. The two Chinese characters used for chikara kurabe may simply represent a general term for combat between two strong men.

In fact there is a complicated story here because the Chinese character (ideograph) for 'compare' can also be read as 'horn'. This may have a connection with Emperor Huang Ti (the Yellow emperor) of about 2500BC who defeated the barbarians who wore horned helmets which they used to pierce their enemy. Thereafter this method was much used in China and also became a sort of game. The characters used for this were 'horn power' and some say this is where the low squat and headfirst charge of modern sumo came from. It could also describe to how deer fight each other especially with the lowered antlers[3].

Sumo as real history emerges from about 400 AD onwards and images of semi-naked wrestlers wearing loincloths can be seen in Korean tomb murals and archaeological objects. So sumo, or *sumai* as it was pronounced then, was the native form of wrestling. The word sumai is derived from the ancient verb sumau meaning to fight or struggle. Sumo has a complicated history which cannot be treated here, but early sumo was clearly used by the warriors as a form of combat training in addition to its ceremonial functions in the Imperial court and in temples and shrines.

Metal technology and the horse

As in most countries the appearance of the horse and the development of metal technology, especially firearms, rapidly changed military science. The horse is recorded as having been introduced to Japan in AD 284 but no doubt there were earlier unrecorded instances of horses being brought to Japan from Korea or China. The use of the horse for hunting and fighting quickly spread among the Imperial court, the aristocracy and the warrior groups. Then for well over a thousand years there was little significant change until the introduction of the musket into Japan by the Portuguese in 1543. Up to this point the chief skills of the Japanese warriors had been for many centuries archery, riding and sword-fighting. The combination of the bow and the horse (*kisha*) combined remarkably well, as can be seen in the victories of the mounted Mongol archers whose hordes spread as far as Europe. After 1543 when the use of firearms quickly spread, the mounted warriors ceased to dominate the battle field since a single bullet could bring down a horse. The early musket had an effective range of about 80 metres.

---

[3] Shortly after writing this I saw some stags fighting in a London park and was struck how like sumo it looked.

Prior to the introduction of the musket, hand-to-hand combat known as kumi-uchi (grappling) or yoroi-kumi-uchi (armoured grappling) was used on the battlefield when weapons were broken, dropped or lost. The armour that the samurai wore provided protection from weapons, from kicks and punches and probably from throws – the stock-in-trade of the later jujitsu schools. One common method of attack in kumi-uchi was to seize projections on the enemy's metal helmet such as the visor and use it to throw him down. A look at the formal techniques of the Koshiki-no-kata of judo which is said to be a kumi-uchi kata taken directly from the Kito style of jujitsu shows how basic these throws were[4].

As in many other countries the native form of wrestling was called upon for physical training and for fighting. In Japan this was sumai (sumo), which in its ancient military form was known as military sumo (*Buke-sumai*) and in its training form as *Renbu sumai*. Buke-sumai flourished during the Kamakura Bakufu (military government) period from 1185 to 1333. The techniques of sumo were already known, as can be seen in the 13th century military romance *Genpei Seisuiki* (The Rise and Fall of the Taira and Minamoto Clans) which mentions the *Shijuhatte* – the traditional list of 48 techniques of Sumai.

Most of these sumai techniques would have been effective in throwing an opponent to the ground where he could then be dispatched. This early sumo was not what we now see on television. It was not fought in a circle nor was it won by forcing the other man out of it and it included throws, kicks and punches. The application of sumai to the combat situation became known as kumi-uchi which means 'grappling'.

Thus the long chain of development to judo was chikara-kurabe – sumai/sumo – kumi-uchi – jujitsu – judo but it was not a straight connection with one form neatly superseding the other. Old arts tend to survive in Japan. Sumo slightly confuses the picture because it was also part of early farming (fertility) festivals[5], Imperial court rituals and festivals and those of the temples and shrines. It had and still has a huge religious and symbolic significance for the Japanese.

---

[4] Kata are formalised and choreographed technique training sequences or drills.

[5] Sumai was also intimately connected to the god of water who was of crucial importance to rice farming.

The introduction of the musket

The introduction of the musket into Japan by the Portuguese in 1543 brought about a number of major changes. Unlike most other martial skills the gun could be quickly mastered and did not require great courage, stamina, size or strength. Thus the guns came to be used by the smaller warriors of which there were plenty. Firearms and cannons also changed the way castles were built and led to the lightening of the cumbersome armour the samurai wore. Since the bullet could penetrate armour the samurai were forced to switch to lighter armour and faster and more nimble movement on the battlefield – wars still had to be fought in the best way possible. The lightening of the armour then gave greater scope for grappling on the battlefield. So in a sense the Portugese hastened the arrival of jujitsu. The horse appeared less and less on the battlefield, which in theory meant more foot-soldiers and hand-to-hand combat, except that the use of the musket in large numbers caused great carnage.

Tokugawa Ieyasu unifies Japan

Up to about 1603 Japan was racked by a very long period of civil wars. This culminated in the complete unification of the country under one man – feudal lord Tokugawa Ieyasu (and his descendants) who imposed a military straitjacket on the country which lasted up to 1868. This created over two hundred and fifty years of peace, an incredibly long period of time. This period is known as the Edo or Tokugawa period. Edo was the old name for Tokyo and this was where the Tokugawa Shogun based himself.

This straitjacket consisted of the isolation of Japan from the outside world, a balanced arrangement of the two hundred and sixty or so friendly and unfriendly formerly feuding clans, a hostage system and the strict division of society into four classes – the samurai warriors, peasant farmers, artisans and merchants. The samurai were in charge and had the legal right to cut down any member of another class for no reason. Within the feudal clans the samurai warriors fulfilled a wide variety of functions from simple soldier to administrator or scholar.

There were however many master-less samurai known as *ronin* (lit. 'wave-men') in the early Edo period (from 1603) who were the flotsam and jetsam of the civil war period prior to unification. The *ronin* were a source of trouble for the Tokugawa authorities but eventually they died out.

Battle scenarios

Some early Japanese battles were decided by the best man or men of one side taking on their counterparts on the other side (*ikki-uchi*) but in the later major battles the weapons with the greatest reach were used first such as the archers and the gunners (often in three lines with each line firing in turn as the others loaded up). The next two lines consisted of long spear and short spear men and then it was down to hand to hand combat with or without swords.

The relative importance of the various martial skills of the samurai can be deduced from the make-up of the armies that fought at the battle of Sekigahara in 1600[6]. A breakdown of 3000 reinforcements sent to Tokugawa Ieyasu by Date Masamune showed that 420 were on horse, 1200 carried firearms, 850 carried spears and 200 carried bows. These and other similar records show that the most important weapons were firearms, followed by spears, then bows, with the sword coming last[7]. The long spears were were used for stabbing or cutting (not throwing) and the skilled archers were used more for sharp-shooting. Most samurai carried two swords whether on foot or on horse.

Before the introduction of the musket, samurai would have been skilled in the main martial arts of sword, bow, and spear and the battlefield would probably have been one huge melee. After the introduction of the gun specialisation began to occur primarily because fire power was best concentrated and had to be protected. As the make up of the army showed most samurai specialised in one weapon but would sword-fight when necessary. As the gun spread the number of casualties increased massively and the need for close combat techniques decreased, although the final stage of any battle must have been hand to hand combat (*hakuheisen*). Note that kumi-uchi was an extension of sword-fighting. If the opponent came close enough the punch, kick, lock or throw would be mixed in where applicable.

Before the word jujitsu emerged in the second half of the 17th century there was a variety of words that denoted aspects of close quarter fighting such as *tai-jitsu* (body techniques), *kogusoku* (halfway between

---

[6] Cf. A History of Japan. Vols. 1-3. By Sansom
[7] Long-spear men standing behind the gunners and archers were often used to protect the front-line gunners and archers from frontal attack.

swordfighting and jujitsu), *tori-te* (catching hold), *yawara* (using the Wa character for *harmony* not the Ju character for *soft*), *kempo* (from the Chinese martial art Chuan-fa), *koshimawari* (hip circling) *hakuda* (from the Chinese *baida* or Shaolin-fist), *shubaku/hobaku* (arrest and binding) and so on, but gradually the word jujitsu came to be used more and more to encompass all the 'non-weapon' techniques. Note that judo, aikido and karate would be regarded by many Japanese martial arts historians as types of jujitsu in so far as they were basically unarmed arts.

Early Edo period jujitsu

Paradoxically it was the very long period of peace in Japan that prepared the ground for the emergence of jujitsu and then a long series of wars from 1894 to 1945 that hastened the development and spread of judo first in Japan and then worldwide.

Jujitsu was not strictly unarmed combat since it featured the use of knives (*tanto*) and other small weapons, and trained in defences against both small and bigger weapons such as the sword. For example one common way that samurai disposed of an enemy was to throw him down and use a knife or a broken arrow to stab through the chinks in his armour. Even after the gun was introduced into Japan the sword remained the notional premier art (*omote-gei*) and jujitsu was an extension of it (*ura-gei*). Jujitsu was something that combined with sword fighting or which you fell back on if you lost your weapons.

However there were other uses of jujitsu which were for those occasions when wearing a sword was prohibited, such as in front of the Emperor, Shogun or other high personage, or for subduing someone who needed to be kept alive for a while. In general relinquishing ones weapons and catching hold of the armed enemy would have been dangerous, especially with other armed enemy around. The Japanese sword is mostly wielded with two hands, so using just one hand to catch hold of the enemy would have been risky. The Japanese peasant farmers may also have learned unarmed combat techniques and minor martial arts such as stick-fighting (jo/bo-jitsu), as did their Chinese counterparts, but they were not allowed to carry swords which would have put them at a disadvantage when facing samurai.

From 1615 the new Tokugawa military ruler of Japan imposed new legal controls on the samurai known as the *Buke Shohatto* (Rules for the

Military) which obliged them to pursue learning and continue their training in the martial arts. This was set out in the first article of the rules and was referred to as *bunbu-ryodo* meaning the dual path of war and literature (the arts of war and the arts of peace). The martial arts in general were referred to by the old term *kyuba no michi* or the way of the horse and bow, which of course included swordsmanship since the samurai and his swords were rarely parted. For centuries the bow, sword and spear were the three main skills of the mounted samurai warriors.

The military ruler Tokugawa Ieyasu had a difficult balancing act to achieve. He needed his men and his allies to stay strong to avoid further civil war and at the same time he could not allow too many samurai or *ronin* to stay idle and possibly foster discontent[8].

From about 1650 the number of compulsory martial arts that the samurai trained in rose to six[9]. They were known as the the six martial arts (*roku-bugei*) and included sword-fighting (*ken-jitsu* or *gekken*), archery (*kyu-jitsu*), horsemanship (*ba-jitsu*), spear-fighting (*so-jitsu*), gunnery (*ho-jitsu*) and hand to hand combat (*jujitsu*). The additions were ho-jitsu (gun) and jujitsu. Surprisingly the word kumi-uchi was not used for hand to hand combat. The word jujitsu started to emerge more and more from about 1650, possibly after being named in one of the later Buke Shohatto law revisions.

As the long and peaceful Edo period continued with no obvious internal or external threats (except perhaps the Christian missionaries and converts) the emphasis shifted to fostering the martial spirit (*shiki*) rather than battlefield skills. This gradually made the various martial arts more formalised and less suited to battlefield reality[10]. One formalisation was the separation of different skills into different martial arts and different – *Ryu* (styles or schools)[11]. In previous times of war the warrior would have required a range of fighting skills which he would mix on the battlefield as appropriate.

---

[8] Samurai is now used as a general term for Japanese feudal warrior. Originally it meant a warrior (bushi) of a particular rank. Ronin is a masterless samurai.

[9] There were many other martial arts. One list numbers the martial arts at eighteen.

[10] Cf Nippon Budo Zenshu Vol 5.

[11] -Ryu means style or school (but not school in the sense of a building).

Jujitsu and kenjitsu schools began practising wearing loose wide-sleeved kimonos and practising on smooth dojo floors or on mats in their bare feet. (In more warlike times no warrior would have gone on the battlefield in his bare feet). One effect of this improvement in training conditions was that these arts became more technical, but it is debatable whether that meant they were more effective on the battlefield. Training was mostly done through kata which might be long and somewhat out of date. Inevitably those with real battlefield experience died away. Despite the fact that the musket was the most effective weapon its practise languished somewhat, since no great martial spirit or fitness was gained by gunnery training.

As Shogun Tokugawa Ieyasu imposed his controls, schools and dojos were required for the samurai in each of the many clans. It was unlikely that they needed much coaxing since for many of them there was little else to do and training facilities would probably have existed already. The position of a clan martial arts teacher was usually hereditary with the father passing on the job to his son. The pressure was on the son to gain as many certificates (*menjo*) as possible in other martial arts and from reputed masters in order to inherit the job! If a son was not up to the job a capable youth could be adopted as a son.

It is estimated that by the end of the Edo period there were something like 179 recorded styles of jujitsu and over 750 styles of sword-fighting[12]. This sounds like a large number of jujitsu styles but there were many clans each training their own men in the way they thought best, and of course many a 'new' style would have been an offshoot of an established style and master. A handful of early styles emerged between 1550 and 1650. The majority of styles thereafter emerged between 1650 and 1750. The statistics here disguise the fact that single martial arts were not necessarily done in specialist dojos. A clan instructor would teach a variety of arts in his clan dojo of which jujitsu would be one. His job was to produce all-round capable samurai.

About 1532 the first recognised 'jujitsu' school – the Takeuchi-ryu – emerged, although it did not describe what it did as jujitsu. It used the terms *kogusoku* and *koshi-mawari*. Kogusoku means literally 'sword

---

[12] Cf. Nippon Budo Zenshu. Vols. 1 & 5.

accoutrements/fittings' and Koshi-mawari means 'round the hips', which sounds like a throw. Kogusoku was regarded as a half way house between kenjitsu and jujitsu. This was still the time when armoured battlefield clashes (yoroi-kumi-uchi) were common and in the military romance literature of the time there are a number of detailed accounts of mounted samurai crashing into each other and trying to cut off the other's head, or crashing down between their horses and trying to finish each other off with short bladed weapons.

After the Takeuchi-ryu a small number of other jujitsu styles emerged, such as Kyushin-ryu of 1558-70, Araki-ryu of about 1590, Seigo-ryu, Sekiguchi Shinshin-ryu, Asayama Ichiden-ryu, Fujiyama-ryu, Yoshioka-ryu and Koguri-ryu all of about 1620. Next was the Yoshin-ryu of about 1640. Note that exact dates for these styles are not known.

Around 1625 three ronin began training under a Chinese boxing (*Chuan Fa*) teacher called Chin Gen-pin. This 'boxing' is known as *Kempo* in Japanese. They were Isogai, Fukuno and Miura who all went on to found their own jujitsu styles some of which later sub-divided. For more on this see Chapter 1 – Chinese Influence.

The Kenjitsu/gekken (sword) schools or styles emerged ahead of jujitsu, mostly during the Muromachi period (1338-1573). The earliest was the Nen-ryu style from about 1350. Since sword fighting and grappling mix it is safe to assume that battlefield grappling dates back to at least that time if not well before since it must always have been part of combat. The famous Shinkage-ryu which included *Muto* or swordless techniques (= grappling?) was founded by Yagyu about 1571.

The emergence of martial arts styles seems to be peculiar to Japan. Europe for example had many fine swordsmen who lived or died by their swords but there was not a huge proliferation of fencing styles. After all there can only be so many ways of using a sword. A good European swordsman might set up his own fencing school to pass on his knowledge and perhaps make a living but that was all. It may have been the rigid Japanese separation into feudal clans, each with their own school that hastened the emergence of the styles. The martial arts master in each clan would have needed to distinguish himself in some way.

The teachers in the clan schools had to be good – they might get challenged at any time – and it was up to them to devise their own systems and training methods to produce capable samurai for their clans. About

80% of the clans had a unique jujitsu style. A small number of clans used the same style[13]. It was by beating challengers that the clan teachers or their top students proved their worth. The real battlefield tests stopped around 1600 with the battle of Sekigahara.

The technical and theoretical principles of jujitsu

In addition to actual combat technique it was common for oriental martial arts schools to have technical and theoretical/spiritual principles. Jujitsu (and judo) used the classical Chinese word **ju** meaning soft (as opposed to hard) to show their core principles and signify their pedigree[14]. What this described was the yielding quality of softness. So Jujitsu could better be translated as *techniques of yielding* and ju–do as the *way of yielding*. If the opponent pushes the other yields to the push and uses it, likewise with a pull.

Ju in classical Chinese could simply be used as an adjective as in 'soft cushion' but from the time of the ancient divination classic *I-Ching* or *Book of Changes* the concept of **ju** was regarded more favourably than **go** meaning hard or resistant. One *I-Ching* section talks about opposites being contained within each other or being reflections of each other like two sides of a coin – soft is hard, weak is strong etc. Water was said to be soft yet it can sweep away mighty rocks. This playing with opposites was a feature of metaphysical logic elsewhere

However the main origin of the martial arts word **ju** comes from a line in the 12th century BC Chinese military classic *San Lueh* (Jap. Sanryaku) meaning the Three Strategies which was written by Chang-liang of the Han Dynasty[15]. In it he writes *Ju yoku go sei(suru)* which means 'the yielding can overcome or defeat the hard or resistant'[16]. This was likened to snow on the willow branch, which bends to shed its load rather than breaking like the pine. Most of the jujitsu schools many centuries

---

[13] The Tenjinshinyo style which Kano studied was one of them.

[14] See Giles' classical Chinese – English dictionary. Many Chinese characters have multiple meanings but in the case of Ju the definition is curt and simple – 'Ju means soft (as opposed to hard)'

[15] The Japanese adopted the Chinese characters to write with in the 8th century AD but they pronounced the characters quite differently.

[16] This is the Japanese reading of the sentence.

later took this line to illustrate their key technical principle. This was later paraphrased as the art of using the enemy's strength to defeat him although in reality it was more a case of using the enemy's movement. Another common jujitsu concept was to avoid the enemy's strength and attack his weaknesses, such as in Atemi strikes to the vital spots, which was not the same thing as using his strength. *Yield and use* would perhaps be a good translation of the concept of **Ju**.

Judo has often been described as the 'gentle art'. In so far as yielding to the enemy's push is relatively gentle it is perhaps an apt translation but gentleness has connotations in English that go beyond yielding. Judo/jujitsu itself is rarely gentle. However the phrase has stuck and perhaps it contributed to judo's early growth among those looking for an art that uses intelligence and minimal force to defeat violence.

Kano himself demolished the concept of using the enemy's strength to defeat him when he wrote that **Ju** was more a defensive concept which did not apply in situations such as when the wrist was already gripped or when seized from behind. In this situation the weak point of the grip had to be worked on. He went on to say that here the superior principle of *Seiryoku Zenyo* (best use of mind and body) had to be applied.

However the idea of using the enemy's strength as being the way a smaller, weaker person can beat a bigger stronger one obviously gripped the imagination everywhere and helped contribute to the spread of jujitsu and judo worldwide.

In the Later Han dynasty of China, around the first century AD, the two character word Jou-tao (Japanese: Ju-do) is found in the chronicles of Emperor Kuang Wu, but here it does not refer to any martial art but means the principle of having a compliant, yielding *attitude* which Kano also valued. (See Chapter 11)

Chinese influence

So far in this history of Judo I have not said much about China, but this huge country with its much older civilisation exerted a powerful influence on Japan in many ways. Luckily, perhaps, Japan was sufficiently far enough away from China to escape its immediate influence being over three hundred miles away by sea. China does not seem to have had a huge martial arts influence on Japan. This may be because the Japanese have always been a warlike race well able to look after themselves. As mentioned above there is one reference in the *Nihonshoki*, which was written in Chinese, to *Shuwaijiao* (said to be like sumai, judo, kumi-uchi) although the two characters used (compare/horn and power) may just be a blanket term for grappling. Japanese sumo seems to be a truly native Japanese wrestling style. Later on there are some mentions of *Kempo* (Chuan-fa or Fist-method) and *Hakuda* (*baida* or Shaolin temple boxing) in Tokugawa-period jujitsu and later to karate of the Ryukyu islands which were much closer to China.

One major difference between Japanese and Chinese weaponry was the Japanese use of the curved sword which was mainly used for cutting as opposed to piercing. This sword was wielded with *two* hands and was reckoned to provide more power but it eliminated other possibilities such as shield (buckler) and sword fighting, or using one arm to grapple or strike with. One famous Japanese warrior called Miyamoto Musashi fought wielding two swords but he and a few others were exceptions.

There is one hiccup in the official jujitsu history. According to the *Honcho Bugei Sho Den* (A Short Account of Japanese Martial Arts) published in 1716, the Chinese Chin Gen-Pin (1587-1671) came to live in Japan in about 1620, where he taught Chuan-Fa Chinese Boxing (*Kempo*) to three Japanese ronin Miura, Fukuno and Isogai, who later went on to found their own jujitsu schools.

This was said by the Honcho Bugei Shoden to be the beginning of jujitsu in Japan, and this was believed for a long time, but later research does not confirm this. For a start there was the much earlier Takeuchi style of jujitsu of around 1530, the Muto (swordless) techniques of the Shinkage-ryu (1570), the Araki-ryu and the Kyushin-ryu all predating Chin Gen-Pin. Also Chin Gen-Pin was a reputed poet and potter who may not have been that good at Chuan-fa since he only trained for thirteen months at the Shaolin temple in China. He eventually went to live in Nagasaki, became Japanese and led a cultured life. Although the fit is not very good he is generally believed to have taught Miura, Fukuno and Isogai and added to the kumi-uchi and kogusoku technique of the time. From the Fukuno school sprang the Teishin-ryu, Jikishin-ryu and the Kito school which was studied by Jigoro Kano and formed part of his judo.

In addition to the basic technical principle of **ju** martial arts teachers often described the theoretical principles of their arts in Buddhist,

Confucian or Taoist terms. Much depended on the orientation of the individual teacher. Generally speaking the Confucians and the 'Strategists'used their martial arts for building up a person or a country (*hito-zukuri* and *kuni-zukuri*), while the specialist martial artists such as the swordsmen were more Buddhistic in their exploration of the mind and the search for 'truth'[17]. Other reasons for the use of these abstract concepts were to give respectability and pedigree to the martial arts and to show concurrence with the beliefs of their rulers.

Correct pedigree or lineage was very important in preserving the integrity and purity of the style. Most schools kept genealogical records of their masters and of those who received the *Menkyo Kaidan* (certificate of complete mastery of the art). It was not uncommon for bogus bujitsu-ka to claim qualification and descent from ancient masters and some even went to so far as to copy the scrolls or manuscripts of a famous style word for word. Sometimes bogus styles were created using a similar-sounding name of a famous style but written with slightly different characters. It was not uncommon to use ancient Chinese philosophers as a source of theoretical wisdom in the quest to appear technically and spiritually profound.

There was another strand which was the health-promoters (*Yojo-ka*) who did *Yojo-jitsu*. They leaned towards Chinese Taoism and aimed to make their martial art double as a form of health-giving exercise leading to a long life. They tended toward the medical side of the martial arts and would have been familiar with Chinese medicine, diet, acupuncture, shiatsu and moxibustion etc, and the internal (*Chi-gung*) breathing and external muscle training exercises known collectively as *Lian Gong* in Chinese or *Renko* in Japanese. For many martial arts teachers it would have been shameful not to be able to treat a sick or wounded student. This early interest in the health side of the martial arts pre-dates Western ideas of physical education but ties in loosely with judo's later physical education objective.

There were no rules to the kumi-uchi or jujitsu techniques used in battle. Nothing was prohibited and the different types of jujitsu technique could be mixed in any way required. Any joint could be wrenched,

---

[17] The Japanese for strategy is '*heiho*'.

dislocated or broken, blows of all sorts were used on any part of the body, throws could be on to any part of the body (head face or shoulder) or combined with arm-locks, restraints were on face-down opponents or those lying on one side and so on. In the last resort the various martial arts of the time were mixed and used as appropriate on the battlefield and were not necessarily separated out individually. Obviously a spear man would have to fight a swordsman as best he could and kumi-uchi would have been part of that mix.

This absence of rules is perhaps the defining feature of jujitsu *vis-a-vis* judo. Once a jujitsu style starts to encompass free fighting with rules, no matter how few, it begins to follow judo's development. Some martial arts historians make the distinction between *bu-jitsu* which was more focused on battlefield technique and the later *Bu-do* (see page 42) which had somehow risen up the spiritual ladder and turned into a spiritual Way (*Do*) because it had become a more refined and technical martial art. However, many of the earlier *Bujitsu-ka* would have disputed this, especially those with Buddhist, Taoist or Confucian leanings and especially those who lived or died by the sword. They would say that coming to terms with death was the ultimate test. See Chapter 9 under Budo and Bushido for more on this.

Kano wrote that before the Meiji Restoration of 1868 the majority of jujitsu-ka only did kata training[18]. After the Restoration crude forms of free-fighting were gradually introduced into the training. In his experience, said Kano, jujitsu was mainly *atemi* (striking techniques) and groundwork (a bit like modern cage-fighting perhaps) and that there were not many throws in jujitsu. It was by chance perhaps that Kano began studying with two Jujitsu masters who mixed kata and randori. The fact that ground-fighting was stressed by the late Edo period jujitsu schools indicates a certain departure from reality since groundwork would be an exceedingly dangerous thing to do on the battlefield especially with other armed enemy warriors standing around.

Jujitsu was a somewhat anachronistic martial art. The *Kumi-uchi* or 'grappling' that was prevalent during the centuries of war in Japan up to around 1600 was part of a type of warfare that soon became extinct,

---

[18] Cf Kano Jigoro Chosaku-shu. Vol 3.

namely that of the armoured warrior sitting on his horse wielding his sword and shooting his bow. The introduction of the musket into Japan by the Portuguese around 1550 stopped this type of mounted warfare but as the long peace wore on the warriors continued to train as in the past – as if the gun did not exist.

From what we know of the Meiji period (1868-1912) jujitsu there were a number of jujitsu-ka who were stronger on the ground than the Kodokan men (Imai of the Takeuchi-ryu and Tanabe of the Fusen-ryu for example) but in standing work they were generally weaker. Writer E.J. Harrison, who trained at jujitsu and judo in Japan from 1897, wrote in his book *The Fighting Spirit of Japan* that while his jujitsu teacher was phenomenal on the ground he was no match for the Kodokan masters in standing work. The Kodokan responded by sending their best men to Kyoto to study groundwork and no doubt the jujitsu people worked on their throwing. Eventually the Kodokan judo rules were changed to make it harder to go into groundwork.

Jigoro Kano explained this by saying that it was better to stay on the feet during a fight in order to take on more than one opponent, that throwing work was better for physical development and technically more difficult and that for overall development it was better to get good at throwing first then work on groundwork, rather than the other way round. However this judo idea of staying on one's feet was never specifically written into the rules, which continue to allow a throw to score whether the thrower falls over or not. Neither was there any significant technical development into standing arm locks or combinations of armlocks and throws (as in sumo), which would appear to follow on from the concept of staying on one's feet. However Japanese teachers often stressed that a good throw was when the thrower did not fall down when making it (unless it was a *sutemi-waza*).

A kumi-uchi man, or someone with actual battlefield experience, would probably agree with Kano's stress on throwing although he might wonder how effective throws would be in rice fields or on grassy battlefields If he were able to look into the future and see the spread of hard pavements he might agree that throws were effective as terminating techniques. The perception of the real fighting situation ultimately shapes the dojo martial art.

Samurai training

The Buke Shohatto laws required the Edo period samurai to work on their martial arts but little is known about their actual peacetime training. They were required to practise the six martial arts, including military science, and study the Confucian Chinese classics, but what did that actually mean in practice? If one sits down and tries to draw up a monthly training programme, difficulties quickly arise. For example were they regularly required to practise *all* martial arts or did they specialise in one or two? Was much expertise gained by working on all six martial arts on a daily basis? Was the training more for the young ones and less for the older ones? Obviously the training would suit the younger ones with specific military jobs such as castle guard but what about the older, more unfit ones or those with non-military jobs to do? No doubt practical considerations would have prevailed.

Furthermore the hostage system (*Sankinkotai*) ensured that for long periods the feudal lord and his retainers or their families would have to be in Edo under the watchful eye of the Shogun and his secret police (*Metsuke*). Each year or in alternate years they could go back to their castle towns leaving their wives and children in Edo, but this considerable disruption and expense must have affected the training of their retainers.

However, certain martial arts combine in battle and may well have been practised together in training. Riding, sword-fighting and archery combined well till the gun came along. Sword-fighting and kumi-uchi/jujitsu combine; however, from a technical viewpoint the principles of sword-fighting, spear-fighting and the other weapon arts are similar, and it is quite likely that weapon training sessions may well have covered two or more of them. Swordsmanship was obviously for close quarter work and the grappling was an extension of that. In terms of its military usefulness unarmed combat probably stood at the bottom of the martial arts food chain[19]. The emergence of the revolver about 1836 would have made unarmed combat even less important. When foreigners began appearing at Japanese ports armed with revolvers they noted the immediate Japanese interest in them.

---

[19] When I was a soldier we did unarmed combat and bayonet fighting but very little compared with weapon training.

Finally one has to consider the length of time it takes to get good at the various martial arts. Jujitsu and kenjitsu take several years of intensive practise. The grappling martial art would also favour the bigger stronger samurai. If you were a *daimyo* (feudal lord) training up your army you would not want your men to train at one martial art for too long. Luckily for the feudal lords shooting was a skill quickly acquired by smaller and less physical samurai.

This, though, is to treat the object of the exercise as the acquisition of martial skills, but as the long peace wore on the objective switched to fostering martial spirit, and this was where the samurai may soon have learned that training at sword-fighting gave the participants a good physical, rough workout, especially with the use of the wooden sword made of oak (*bokken/bokuto*) which could easily crack a skull. The invention of the lighter bamboo sword (*shinai*) around 1752 also helped develop the kenjitsu equivalent of free-fighting. Jujitsu may well have followed this route but first it had to separate from sword-fighting. Then it could be practised as an unencumbered grappling style.

One modern jujitsu master wrote that there were very few specialist jujitsu dojos before the *Haito* Order of 1876 which banned the carrying of swords[20]. However that ban takes us very close to the founding of Kodokan judo in 1882. If most of the Han (feudal domain) dojos did not specialise in jujitsu one wonders how much time was spent on it and how good the jujitsu could have been. Possibly there were never more than a few centres of strong jujitsu at any time. The difficulties that Kano Jigoro, the founder of judo, encountered in finding a jujitsu teacher in Tokyo (Edo) is perhaps a reflection of this, especially when you consider that in theory all the 260 or so clans had jujitsu teachers and many students.

One important factor not to be overlooked is that despite the increasing formalisation of the martial arts during the Edo period there was, it seems, a lot of reality-testing of the martial arts. In sword-fighting, unofficial duelling known as *tsuji-kiri* (*crossroad cutting*) and in jujitsu *tsuji-nage* (*crossroad throwing*) took place as did matches between dojos (*taryu-jiai*). Certain known crossroads were where such action often happened.

There was also the practice known as *musha-shugyo* where individual samurai travelled around looking for top teachers to study under or

---

[20] Cf. Jujitsu Kyohan by Anegawa.

challenge. Additionally there was a common practice known as *dojo-arashi* (dojo-storming) or *dojo-yaburi* (dojo-breaking) where warriors toured the dojos and challenged the top man or men. Also many samurai had an over-sensitive sense of honour and spontaneous duels and brawls to the death were fairly common.

Budo

In addition to the technical and theoretical principles of the individual martial arts there was also the parallel development of the samurai ethos namely *Budo* (the Military Way) or the later word *Bushido* (the Way of the Warrior). The history of Japan before 1600 was one of almost five hundred years of intermittent warfare. The warrior ethos centred on loyalty to a feudal lord (or the Emperor) and bravery in battle and the Japanese attitude to death sat squarely in the middle of this. Fighting was usually to the death with no surrender (capturing for ransom was not very common and if it did happen, the fate of the individual was pretty gruesome, which in itself was enough to keep them fighting), and if an individual did something shameful he was expected to kill himself by *seppuku* – ritual suicide by cutting the stomach[21]. Individually the samurai led spartan, frugal lives and looked down upon commerce. Yet at the same time the somewhat Confucian laws for the military (Buke Sho Hatto) obliged them to study, which many did. Later original Japanese thinkers were often from the samurai class. See Chapter 9 for more on Budo and Bushido.

---

[21] The usual practice was for the individual to start the stomach cut then an assistant lopped off his head with a sword.

Chapter 2
The Emperor Returns – the Shogun Falls
1868

By their very nature the samurai were an unproductive class only necessary in time of war, whereas the farmers, artisans and merchants had specific and productive roles. Arai Hakuseki, a noted Japanese scholar of the 17th century, wrote that barely one in ten of the samurai had sufficient arithmetic or writing to make them employable. Over the long period of peace the samurai became increasingly poor, the merchants became richer and the system imposed by the Tokugawa clan became increasingly irrelevant. Quite early on there were instances of samurai taking up trades which would bring in some money and even selling their status, usually by way of marriage or adoption, to a non-samurai, despite the fact that movement into and out of the samurai class was forbidden.

From about 1800 the power of the Tokugawa military government slowly ebbed away. This was caused by a number of factors such as the hostility of the Imperial court in Kyoto, the antagonism of the powerful western (Kyushu) clans, natural disasters such as famine, the widespread discontent of the oppressed farmers and the general irrelevance of the system to the society of the time. The needy samurai became more focused on scraping a living for themselves and their families. The Americans and British came knocking on the door with their gun-ships and eventually the seclusion policy was abandoned.

The forceful opening of Japan came as a great shock to this warlike nation led by samurai, for there was very little they could do about it. It was obvious to most, but not all samurai, that swordmanship was not the answer – warships and modern technology were.

In due course the Tokugawa military government collapsed without major civil war breaking out and in 1868 the Imperial government under Emperor Meiji was restored. The last time an Emperor ruled was when Emperor Godaigo ruled in the 14th century. The new Imperial government promoted a series of measures to dissolve the four class system (warrior, merchant, artisan and farmer) which had been in place since

1603 and to strip the warrior (samurai) class of its special privileges. In 1876 the new government forbade the samurai from wearing their distinctive clothes and hairstyle (topknot) and more importantly from carrying swords. Along with this went a ban on sword-fighting as a training exercise. One other thing the new government brought in was a conscript army composed of ordinary citizens, many of whom were of non-samurai origin, and they quickly proved that they were equally as good as the samurai class. This was yet another blow to the samurai pride.

Japan begins to modernise

Japan recognised the pressing need to modernise itself not only in order to stand up to the aggressive Western military powers such as America, Russia and Britain, but to rank among the world's nations as a modern country. It swiftly and relentlessly embarked on this course and the privileges of the samurai class were amongst the early casualties. Most samurai, though not all, knew that this was the way to go and did not oppose it. Luckily for the country, over 250 years ago Tokugawa Ieyasu had required them to continue their education and polish their martial spirit. They formed the backbone of the new government.

Thrown out of work, so to speak, the samurai had more urgent things to attend to such as providing for their families, and the martial arts looked as if they might disappear forever, not only as methods of fighting but as physical training exercises. The Meiji government did make some efforts to assist impoverished samurai but these mostly failed since its grasp of modern economics was not sophisticated enough.

About this time the martial artists were also out of favour. Public fights between sumo wrestlers and jujitsu men were often staged for money and some samurai put on public shows of their martial arts skills, also for money. Popular fiction of the time often described the martial artists (bujitsu-ka) as villains. One reason for their loss of popularity was their involvement in the Saga and the Shimpuren rebellions of the early Meiji period, which violently opposed the new policies of the government. "Those who practise gekken should be regarded as national criminals," said one governor of Kyoto, and the practice of swordsmanship was banned. Some swordsmen who opposed the sword ban ventured outdoors with their swords hidden in a sack slung over the shoulder. A few of them continued promoting the old arts and practising in private.

Sumo too suffered from the modernisation fervour of the time. At the height of the modernisation boom sumo wrestlers (*rikishi*) were described in one Japanese newspaper as fat naked men who should be banned since they projected such an antiquated image of Japan. One group of rikishi even created a fire brigade for local people to raise their popularity. Eventually the Emperor noticed sumo's plight and in 1872 and 1881 he attended two sumo events which reaffirmed Imperial approval.

From Jujitsu to Judo – the Early Shoots

1877 marks the year when young Jigoro Kano began studying at Tokyo Imperial University and enrolled with Fukuda Hachinosuke, a teacher of the Tenjinshinyo style of jujitsu. After over four years of jujitsu training he set up his own dojo in 1882 where he began to teach what he called Kodokan Judo. Kano's early motivation was to learn how to protect him self from bullying which he had experienced at school, but the more he taught the more he realised that a modified jujitsu would make a fine physical training method and competitive exercise.

Kano was not completely alone. At about the same time that Kano was establishing his dojo there were others thinking along the same lines. For instance about 1877 jujitsu practice began to appear in certain middle schools[22]. Also after the demonstration of the superiority of its *Batto-tai* (sword unit) during the Seinan revolt of 1874 the Tokyo Metropolitan Police (*Keishicho*) thought about the content of its training and adopted Gekken (fencing) and jujitsu for police training. According to police records the Shinto-ryu jujitsu school had two strong men – and flourished up to and into the Meiji period. In 1883 the Keishicho singled out three of Shinto-ryu's best men to teach jujitsu to the police. This was perhaps the first adoption of jujitsu by an official body for practical modern purposes. The Keishicho thereafter went on to play a prominent role in the history of judo.

A German Tokyo University medical lecturer, Dr. Baelz, was also active in promoting jujitsu and gekken for exercise purposes about the same time. Baelz, unlike Kano, did not run a dojo, but at a time when the Japanese were distancing themselves as quickly as they could from their old

[22] Cf. Oimatsu's Judo Gojunen (Fifty years of Judo).

arts the fact that an influential foreigner such as Baelz was not only saying that these arts were valuable but was practising them as well must have made many Japanese think again[23]. See below for more on Baelz.

The immediate political background to this was Order 399 of the Council of State in 1871 banning the wearing of a sword, the practice of fencing and the banning of the other distinguishing marks of the samurai such as their clothing and hairstyle. Again in 1876, Order 38 of the Council of State decreed that the only groups that could wear a sword outdoors were the police and the army in the execution of their duties. Other than that it was strictly forbidden and those who contravened this law would have their swords confiscated.

With the banning of the sword it looked like the traditional martial arts would disappear entirely. Despite the modernisation fervour of the time some former samurai opposed this and looked for means to reintroduce these arts either as martial arts and/or forms of exercise.

In 1872 a new education system was laid down. The new curriculum included physical training (*taiso*) but it was the foreign physical jerks type training that was used. This was soon felt to be monotonous and was disliked by the former samurai class. They pushed for the introduction of the martial arts, as taught in the old Han schools, into the new schools and in 1883 the Ministry of Education initiated an investigation into kenjitsu/gekken and jujitsu.

The Ministry of Education team that first investigated jujitsu and gekken consisted of Shibukawa Hangoro of the Shibukawa style of jujitsu, Tomita Shojiki and Hisatomi Tetsutaro. This team was later expanded to include medical investigation by three medics, namely Dr Miyake who was head of the Tokyo university medical school and two foreign medics, Dr Elwin Baelz (see above) and Dr Julius Schrieber, also from the medical school. Instead of looking only at the Shibukawa style of jujitsu they investigated Tenjinshinyo, Toda and Kito styles of jujitsu. Dr Baelz's son records in his book that his father was active in promoting Sakakibara style Kenjitsu and Totsuka Yoshin style jujitsu and that there was a young student, Jigoro Kano, also at Tokyo University, who was actively promoting jujitsu at the time[24].

---

[23] Baelz is said to have treated a number of highly placed members of Japanese society.
[24] "Awaking Japan: The Diary of a German Doctor: 1849-1913". Viking Press 1931.

The investigation when completed listed five benefits and nine disadvantages (violent, aggressive, dangerous etc). The Ministry came down against the formal introduction of these arts into the curriculum but allowed limited introduction where they already existed, particularly in a number of middle schools. Kano had by this time established his Kodokan and had become a teacher at the Gakushuin so it seems fairly likely that he would have been aware of the Ministry of Education investigation and must have pondered on the various benefits and disadvantages of jujitsu and gekken.

In the 16th year of Meiji (1883) the Imperial Rescript on Education was proclaimed. In this largely Confucian Rescript intellectual training (*chi-iku*) and moral training (*toku-iku*) were stressed along with Confucian values, although physical education was not specifically mentioned. As can be seen later Kano Jigoro, the founder of Kodokan Judo, included in his judo system both chi-iku and toku-iku (under one of its three objectives namely *shushin-ho* or moral training), following the general lines of the Imperial Rescript which dominated Japanese education right up to the end of the Pacific War (second world war) in 1945.

If one considers the timing of the Ministry of Education investigation and the Imperial Rescript on Education it would seem quite likely that the young Kano, who had set up his first dojo about one year before, would be heavily influenced in the direction he was to take his judo.

Chapter 3
Kano's Family Background

In order to know more about Kano and the circumstances of the time it is necessary to go back to his birth in 1860 to what was the middle of a dangerous period. Kano Jigoro, the founder of judo, was born in the Kano family home in the village of Mikage in Ubara county, Settsu province (now Hyogo Prefecture, Muko county, Mikage-ward, Kobe-city).

One year before his birth the so-called Ansei Mass Imprisonment occurred. Ii, the Chief Minister of the Shogun (military ruler), confined the court nobles and feudal lords and arrested loyalists whom he punished with death or imprisonment. The loyalists were from the *Sonno-Joi* faction ('Revere the Emperor and expel the foreigners') which opposed Ii's actions in support of the Shogun who was in favour of opening up the country to foreigners. Minister Ii paid for this the following year (1860) in the Sakuradamon Incident where he was murdered by former retainers of the loyalist Mito clan outside the Sakurada Gate as he was about to enter Edo castle.

In 1862 there was also the so-called Namamugi Incident when some British men tried to pass through a procession of the lord of the Satsuma clan and were attacked by sword-wielding samurai, resulting in one dead and two wounded. In retaliation seven British warships bombarded Kagoshima in 1863. The clan later paid an indemnity of 70,000 gold Ryo bars to the British.

These incidents highlighted the growing weakness of the Tokugawa military government (*bakufu*). During this period the military government began to implode, making way for the return of Imperial rule in 1868. It was an anxious and dangerous time for Japan.

The Kano family

Kano Jigoro was the third son and one of five children. The female (Kano) side of the family were originally farmers who switched to making *sake* (rice wine) in 1659 and prospered from then on as *sake* merchants. His father was Kano Jirosaku (Shogenji Mareshiba) who originally came from the priestly Shogenji (Omi Hiei Taisha) family who were in charge of the Great Shinto Shrine of Omi Hiei. His mother was Kano Sadako.

Kano Jigoro was born in the main family home called the Hamahigashi-tei (Eastern Beach Mansion) – which also contained the Senpokaku or Palace of a Thousand Sails – in the pleasant costal farming village of Mikage. The beach by the house was covered with sand, the water was clear and young Kano Jigoro often swam there. The view out to sea was a magnificent one with many sailing ships passing by. The Mikage land was renowned for its Nada sake production from the Edo period onwards when the demand for sake from Edo grew massively. From that time on the Kano sake branch of the family survived various ups and downs but still exists today as the Hon-Kano Shoten Company, producing its quality Kiku Masamune brand. In more modern times heavy development has affected the area, located close as it is to major industrial and commercial areas such as Osaka and Kobe. Unfortunately the Senpokaku no longer exists.

The Kano's Mikage family home was established as a retirement home three generations earlier by Jigoro's great maternal grandfather Jisaku. Kano's father Jirosaku was the second generation to live there. Jisaku was reputedly a genial character who owned twelve sake warehouses and twelve ships. He was well known in the local business world and was well-connected to influential people in the wider Osaka and Kyoto areas. Jigoro's father Jirosaku was adopted by Jisaku who soon recognised his talents and made him his son–in–law and later his heir. Adoption was a common Japanese custom for bringing talent into a family and for perpetuating the family line in the absence of a son and heir.

The Shogenji family

Jirosaku's family history gives a clue to Kano Jigoro's later successes. Jirosaku, born in 1813, was the fourth son of Shogenji Maretake, the hereditary priest of the *Omi Hiei Taisha* (*Omi Hie* Great Shinto Shrine). His oldest brother and third brother both died young leaving the second brother to inherit the priestly position from his father. Jirosaku then set off to seek fame and fortune travelling as far as Nagasaki. He was said to be a brave self-composed character with quasi-political ambitions and a talent for literature, which in those days meant Chinese classics and calligraphy.

Jirosaku occasionally visited Mikage in his early travels and it was not long before he was employed to teach literature to members of the Kano family. Jisaku recognised his character and qualities and eventually received him as an adopted son. Jirosaku then went on to marry one of the daughters, Sadako. Kano Jisaku had a son of his own called Ryotaro, but when he was on his deathbed he gathered all his family around him and made Jirosaku his heir, entrusting him with the family business. Ryotaro, he said, was to set up his own family line. Jirosaku went along with this at the time but after the Buddhist memorial service for his adoptive father he revealed that he intended to resign as head of the house and wanted Ryotaro to take over. He himself would seek his family's fame and fortune elsewhere but his wife and children should stay in their family home. The family as a whole agreed to this solution. Possibly Jirosaku was not content with running a sake business and had his eye on greater things in the capital or maybe he thought Ryotaro had had a raw deal.

According to the Shogenji family records, the family's connection to the Great Shinto Shrine of Hiei in Omi (*Omi Hiei Taisha*) goes back to when Emperor *Tenchi* moved the Imperial capital to the nearby Otsu in AD 668. The very early family history is not absolutely clear but the Emperor's move to Otsu ties in with the family records. (The family also counts among its ancestors such historic figures as Ushimaro and Horibe no Sukune) The Hiei great shrine is famous in Japanese history for being burned down in 1571, along with the Enryaku-ji temple on Mt. Hiei, by Oda Nobunaga, one of the three men who unified Japan[25]. The mountain which overlooks Kyoto was the home to the many warrior monks who threatened the capital. Oda Nobunaga ruthlessly eliminated the base and the monks. The Shogenji family foundered a bit at that point but later revived. Eventually the *Hiei* great shrine was rebuilt in 1586.

One advantage of belonging to a Shinto priestly family was that it did not quite fit into the four class system set up by the Tokugawa military ruler, whereby a person was either a samurai, peasant farmer, artisan or merchant, in that order of importance. Furthermore by administering a famous Shinto shrine it created a connection with the Imperial family which headed the state religion of Shinto.

---

[25] Unification started with Nobunaga and Hideyoshi and was completed by Tokugawa Ieyasu

As is common in Japan, Jirosaku devoted his time almost completely to his work which meant leaving his wife and children (including Jigoro Kano) in their family home in Mikage for very long periods. Unfortunately Kano Jigoro's mother, who he described as having a very strong character, died when he was ten and soon after he joined his father in Tokyo, aged eleven, at his father's house in Kakigara-cho[26]. With the long absences of his father the death of his closest parent at such an early age was a heavy blow. However even at such an early age he is recorded as saying that he wanted to go to Edo (Tokyo) and become famous – like his father perhaps.

Having resigned as head of the Kano family, Jirosaku soon went to work for the *Bakufu* (military government) in its costal maritime freight division (sail and steam) and at the same time he owned and managed some ships himself. The family were obviously well off.

In 1863 the Bakufu's warship administrator Katsu Yasuyoshi (aka Kaishu – a famous Zen and kendo man) was ordered by the Bakufu to construct coastal fortresses at Cape Wada and other strategic spots. Jirosaku co-operated in this project working as a contractor. The Cape Wada fortress was completed the following year. Kaishu as will be seen later was a name that crops up more than once in this book.

In 1867 Jirosaku, along with Bakufu Junior Councillor Nagai and others, proposed starting up the first regular Edo – Osaka – Kobe coastal service for goods and passengers, using Western-style ships which the Bakufu agreed to. This was the first such service in Japan.

When the establishment of trading companies for foreign trade became urgent, permission was gained to open the Hyogo port and Jirosaku was ordered by the Bakufu to take part in the planning of the project and then in various preparations for it. However in June of that year he and nineteen others were invited along to the Kyoto residence of the Shogun Tokugawa Yoshinobu where they were granted various ranks by Shogunal Elder Councillor Itagura and ordered to create Japan's first trading company.

Despite Jirosaku's connection with the old military government he was soon promoted by the new Meiji Imperial government when it took

---

[26] In Japan a child is reckoned to be in his first year at birth and therefore one year old who becomes two after the first twelve months and so on. This is known as kazoedoshi and can cause confusion.

over. It was not long before he joined official circles where he distinguished himself in various projects including commerce, construction, shipbuilding and Imperial palace construction. When he died in 1885, aged seventy-two, he was serving as Chief Secretary to the navy (*Kaigun Kendai Shokikan*). This was just some three years after the founding of the Kodokan when he would have had little idea how famous his son was to become.

One big question regarding Kano Jigoro is how he managed to achieve so much as a young man in a society traditionally run by much older men. His father's ability and work connections provide one answer. Secondly, he came from a wealthy background; thirdly and perhaps most importantly he had connections with the Imperial family through his father's family; and fourthly he became a teacher at the Gakushuin (Nobles College) where in 1887 he helped educate the future Taisho emperor.

The Shogenji Hiei Taisha family, apart from being very ancient, was part of the Shinto state religion which was controlled by the powerful Shrines and Temples Commissioner (Jisha Bugyo), with, of course, the Emperor at its head. Various members of the Shogenji family served the Imperial family directly such as Mareko, who was court lady to the Empress Dowager (Omiya Gosho). She had one child but it died young. Another relative, Sukako, was summoned as Lady in Waiting in 1879, and under the name of Kozue no Meifu (*myo?*) served the Emperor Meiji for many years. Another relative called Sugi Eisaburo worked in the Imperial Household Agency (*Kunaisho*) where he was head of the Imperial Library, Museum and Mausoleums. The young Kano had connections and wealth behind him but he was also young, highly educated with a good command of English and possibly more able than most older Japanese to take Japan into a modern world. In addition, and most unusually, he was an academic who was creating the fastest growing jujitsu school in Japan. This brought him a lot of publicity.

The Shogenji and Kano families cemented the relationships between them with further marriages. Families were large in those days but there were also many early deaths among the children. Arranged marriages and adoption were the norm and were used to spread the family influence either through the male or female line. The Shogenji family also contained Confucian scholars, poets and literary people which accounts in part for Kano's development as an academic and Chinese classical scholar. Kano

Jigoro himself married Takezoe Sumako when he was thirty-two thus establishing a connection with the Takezoe family which included a number of talented people. In the days when social security did not exist, family connections were highly important and well-maintained, particularly in Confucian Japan.

Chapter 4
Young Kano Goes to Tokyo

Kano began studying when he was seven years old under the tutelage of artist Yamamoto and Dr Yamagishi. As with most primary education in Japan in those times he studied calligraphy and the four Chinese Confucian classics[27]. After his mother died he went to Tokyo to live with his father where he continued to study the Chinese classics under one Kizawa till the age of eleven.

From the age of eleven Kano attended a nearby school called Seitatsu Shojuku in Ryogoku where he studied the Confucian classics and calligraphy under Ubukata Keido who was the head of the school. At the same time he commuted regularly to Mizukuri Shuhei's school in Kanda. At the age of fourteen he began boarding at the Ikuei-gijuku which was run by a Dutchman with German lecturers. At this school all the lectures were in English, but since he had worked at English in his first school he was able to keep up with the other students. However he suffered a certain amount of bullying by some of the other students because of his slight physique. He began to think about getting stronger and recalled stories he had heard about Japanese jujitsu which enabled smaller, weaker people overcome bigger, stronger ones. He resolved to study this art.

Among the many people who entered his family Mikage house in Hyogo prefecture was a samurai of *Hatamoto* (bannerman) rank by the name of Nakai, who boasted that he had once trained at jujitsu. He occasionally showed Kano some of the kata. Kano said he would like to learn more jujitsu but Nakai replied that there was now no need to learn it and turned him down. Kano also asked Katakiri, a guard at his father's Tokyo house, about jujitsu and he showed Kano some kata. When Kano asked for more instruction Katakiri also refused, saying that there was no need for it. Kano also tried asking another visitor to the house by the name of Imai who said he had studied the Kyushin-ryu style of jujitsu, but

---

[27] They were known as *Shisho*.

was again turned down. So Kano carried on with his studies, fretting about getting stronger but unable to find anyone to teach him jujitsu.

Enters Tokyo Imperial University

In 1874 Kano passed the entrance examination to the Tokyo Foreign Language School at the age of fifteen and entered the English language section. Fellow students included Kato Takaaiki who later became Foreign Minister a number of times and Tsuboi Kumazo who became a well known historian. It was not long however, before this section was made independent as a government English language school. In 1875 he entered the *Kaisei* School which was a government college established for the study of foreign sciences. This school later merged with the *Tokyo Igaku* (medical school) and the *Tokyo Kobu Gakko* (industrial school) to become the Imperial Tokyo University. In 1878, one year after Tokyo Imperial University was founded, Kano, aged eighteen, enrolled in the faculty of literature.

At Tokyo Imperial University Kano was taught by non-Japanese lecturers such as Fenelosa, Cooper and Hawden, plus other Japanese lecturers. Many of the courses were taught entirely in English. As is still the case today the workload in such universities is ferocious and here it was that Kano noticed how many of the students who sat poring over their books for hours on end looked rather puny and unhealthy. This partially spurred him on in his promotion of judo as a form of physical education.

While at the language school he lived with a number of other students at the house of a friend of his father. As with the *Ikuei-gijuku* there were a number of stronger students from the former clans who tried to rule the roost and Kano was even more aware of his slight physique. His desire to learn jujitsu increased. He asked his father if he could learn from the former jujitsu people who frequented his house but his father would not agree, probably thinking it was now an old-fashioned desire. Nevertheless Kano thought he was of an age when he could make some of his own decisions and began scouring the city for a jujitsu teacher.

Finds a jujitsu teacher

About this time he heard by chance that many of those who formerly taught jujitsu were now practising Japanese osteopathy (*seikotsu*), so whenever he saw a board advertising it he entered and enquired about jujitsu. Many replied that they knew nothing, although there was one who said he did jujitsu before but not any longer. Some time later he saw a sign advertising seikotsu near the Benkei Bridge in Nihonbashi and entered the building to find a white haired but sturdy-looking old man called Yagi Teinosuke. Kano asked him if he did jujitsu and Yagi looked at him sternly and asked him why. Kano explained his desire to learn and begged to be taught. Yagi explained that he was the direct student of the founder of the school – Iso Mataemon – whose jujitsu licence (*menkyo*) he held, and that previously he had taught jujitsu but not any longer. Yagi went on to say that he would like to help Kano but he only had one small eight mat room which Kano could see before him. He thought for a moment about Kano's request then recollected that there was a man called Fukuda Hachinosuke of the same jujitsu school as himself who might still be running a dojo in another part of Nihonbashi. He invited Kano to go and take a look. Kano soon found Fukuda and his tiny dojo, which he combined with a seikotsu business, and began his training in the Tenjinshinyo style of jujitsu in 1877. His long held ambition was about to be realised.

Fukuda was a fortunate choice since it was said he was equivalent to assistant professor of the former military government's Kobusho (martial arts school). There a number of styles of jujitsu were practised of which the strongest was reckoned to be the Yoshin-ryu style.

Fukuda had just a few students. There were four or five who came occasionally to train, one who came every day and one who came every other day. Sometimes Kano was the only student there and was ordered to do solo practice (*hitori geiko*). Young Kano soon learned that Fukuda was not slow to use his stick on him if he idled. Kano began going regularly, learning the kata from Fukuda and practising them with another student. After that he did randori (free-fighting) with the two of them without rest. Kano was so hooked on his training that he quickly picked up many grazes and his body was soon covered in plasters, but his technical ability developed very rapidly. The Tenjinshinyo style of jujitsu taught by Fukuda developed from an amalgam of the Yoshin-ryu and the Shin no Shinto-ryu under its founder Iso Mataemon. It concentrated on atemi striking techniques and groundfighting and the link between the two was a small number of basic throwing techniques. This became more obvious when Kano later began studying the Kito style of jujitsu, which specialised in throwing.

Kano relates how a jujitsu-ka of the Miura-ryu entered the Fukuda dojo one day and issued a loud, rude challenge to Kano who at the time was the only one there. This was in the old tradition of dojo-yaburi or dojo destruction. Kano was minded to take him on but knew at the time he was not the strongest in the dojo and that if he lost to this man it would adversely affect the dojo's reputation. So he told the man that he would arrange something with the other pupils and asked him to return later. However the Miura man failed to show up.

Kata was the main method of practising jujitsu and most of the other martial arts. Kata, meaning form, was and is very important in Japan. The kata acted as information bases and in them the teacher tried to capture the basics (*kihon*) of his art. Most teachers taught privately to their students and the techniques were kept secret to add to their efficiency. New students were expected to memorise the Kata since illustrated manuals were not usually made available. This secrecy became one of the later differences between jujitsu and judo, which was taught in a very public way. Some jujitsu schools had many techniques which required considerable memorisation. The Yoshin-ryu school had 303 techniques for example. (See also Chapter 9 – The Establishment of the Butokukai Kata). The emphasis laid on kata varied from teacher to teacher. Some teachers thought that kata alone was all that was needed to learn their martial art while others introduced small amounts of free-fighting, but according to Kano this introduction of free-fighting was quite late in the day – from about the time of the Restoration of Imperial rule in 1868.

With, for example, the premier martial art of sword fighting or indeed with any of the weapon martial arts it would not be possible to fight realistically since training partners might quickly die out. So the sword teachers created slow technique sequences that could not be varied for safety's sake, and later on used bamboo or wooden swords. The same applied to jujitsu but to a lesser degree, since many of the techniques were not immediately lethal. This way the trainees could work on a variety of moves in safety.

Another small consideration with the weapons was that they were the product of long hours of a smith's labour when made in the traditional way. The blades were extremely sharp, unlike the European rapier which was mainly used for piercing, but if one sharp edge met another sharp edge one or both expensive blades might be ruined.

As noted before, jujitsu and kenjitsu were reality-tested in matches between schools and in brawling and duels. Duels often happened for relatively trivial reasons. For example if the scabbards of two samurai happened to touch in public that could spark off a fight to the death. Whether the average samurai experienced many of these real fights (*shinken-shobu*) is not known. Since the outcome of this reality-testing might be fatal for either party it must have been fairly self-limiting. In the case of ken-jitsu/gekken, free-fighting (randori) methods using wooden or bamboo swords evolved earlier to enable the trainees to train more realistically and more intensely.

Fukuda was a very traditional jujitsu teacher. Once, Kano was thrown by him with Sumi-gaeshi and stopped to ask about the technique. Fukuda said nothing but threw him again and then again when Kano repeated the question. Fukuda's method was to make Kano learn from experience not from words.

In 1879 Fukuda died aged 52. In the Fukuda dojo there were others stronger in randori than Kano, but Kano's ability in kata and randori together was greater and he was the keenest of all the students in his attendance. Because of this Kano was given all the manuscripts and scrolls (*densho*) of the school by the Fukuda family and entrusted with the dojo. Strictly speaking Jigoro Kano did not receive his Menkyo licence from Fukuda before he died, but in reality he was his successor. Before Fukuda died he and Kano were invited to demonstrate jujitsu to a high ranking foreign visitor.

Demonstrates jujitsu to former US President Ulysses S. Grant

Perhaps because of interest expressed by US President Ulysses Grant in some of the old martial arts, or perhaps because the Japanese wanted to show off their martial skills[28], jujitsu experts including Iso Masatomo and Fukuda Hachinosuke and students Fukushima and Kano Jigoro, were invited by industrialist and senior government official Shibusawa Eiichi to perform a demonstration of jujitsu before the former president and the Shogun when Grant visited Japan in 1879.

---

[28] When the Comodore Perry arrived in Japan in 1853-54 with his 'Black ships' to pressure Japan to conclude a treaty with America, sumo wrestlers were deliberately used to carry heavy rice bales to impress the Americans. It was said that some rikishi carried two or more bales while two or more American sailors struggled to carry one.

Ulysses S.Grant was the 18th president of the United States and was one of the leading generals of the American Civil War, which has been described as the first of the great modern wars. Perhaps his greatest victory as a soldier was the capture of Vicksberg. He was generally regarded as a great soldier and strategist and no doubt had a professional interest in jujitsu.

The demonstration was performed at the Shibusawa residence at Mt Asuka. Kano assisted with the randori exhibition and was perhaps an obvious choice since he could explain to Grant in English what it was all about.

Kano continued his training at the Fukuda dojo for a while but did not have the confidence to go it alone. His desire to take his jujitsu up to another level gradually strengthened. So he joined another dojo run by Iso Masatomo a student of the original founder of the Tenjinshinyo style whom he knew from the Grant demonstration. Along with him went Fukushima Kenkichi, a sturdy fellow student of the Fukuda dojo and former fisherman. At the time Iso Masatomo was already about sixty years old. He did not give instruction in free-fighting but was renowned for his kata teaching. The free-fighting he entrusted to two assistants, Sato and Muramatsu. However, since both Kano and Fukushima had done quite a lot of free-fighting in the Fukuda dojo they both became assistants and alternated with Sato and Muramatsu.

Attendance at the Iso dojo was generally much better than at the Fukuda dojo but since Sato and Muramatsu tended not to attend very regularly Kano more often than not ran the session alone starting with kata, following up with randori with each of the students. Iso Masatomo told Kano a story which perhaps was influential in later directing his judo along the path of stressing throwing techniques and restricting groundwork. One day three jujitsu-ka came to challenge him (dojo-yaburi) at his dojo which Iso accepted there and then. However, they fanned out and came at him simultaneously with atemi strikes, which laid him flat.

After the sessions Kano frequently returned home late and very exhausted, so much so that he occasionally fell over, hitting the roadside fences. His new teacher Iso Masatomo was not a big man and in his youth had not made a name for himself in free-fighting although his knowledge of kata was of the best. Kano learned a lot of kata from this teacher but not a lot about randori, which he hardly taught. In 1881 Iso Masatomo died aged 62. Kano now had to look for a new teacher for the third time.

Luckily he managed to find his third teacher through the good offices of the father of a fellow Tokyo University student called Motoyama. Motoyama was a good friend of Kano and the two often went rowing, or played baseball or went on trips to the mountains etc. Motoyama's father had previously worked in the Kobusho (Martial Arts College) of the military government and recommended an instructor called Iikubo Tsunetoshi of the *Kito* style of jujitsu who was apparently very good. Despite the fact that this jujitsu style was different, Kano was eager to be taught. This time he had chosen a style which concentrated on throwing and he had a master who was still good at free-fighting. Kano began studying under Iikubo Tsunetoshi in July of 1881 and eventually gained his licence (menkyo) and certificate of mastery in the art (Menkyo Kaidan) in 1883.

Becomes a *Gakushuin* teacher

Kano's studies at Tokyo Imperial University continued and in 1881 Kano graduated from the faculty of literature in both politics and economics[29]. The faculty of literature at the time was divided into four sections – politics, economics, philosophy and a combined Japanese and Chinese studies section. The students could either follow the Japanese and Chinese section or any two of the other sections for three years. Kano however decided to stay on for a further year's study of philosophy[30].

In 1882 while Kano was pursuing this extra year's study at Tokyo University, a new study course was set up in the Nobles College (*Gakushuin*), and Kano was asked to lecture there in politics and economics at the age of twenty-three. One of the reforms of the new Imperial government was to abolish the old four-class feudal system and introduce a three-class system consisting of the nobility, ex-military and the common people (who still remained somewhat oppressed but with far fewer restrictions than before). The Nobles College was set up to educate the sons of the aristocracy. By all accounts they were an unruly bunch

---

[29] Eventually there were six imperials universities including Kyoto.

[30] Some accounts say that the extra year's study was of ethics and aesthetics but they might have been part of the philosophy course which included Eastern philosophy.

with very different degrees of intelligence and ability and, being mostly rich kids, were somewhat indifferent to education.

During his time at the College Kano was not inclined to tolerate idle aristocratic children. He worked hard to include talented boys of all classes and more or less knocked the college into shape. Kano started off as a lecturer in his special subjects but soon became an official of the institute which meant he became involved in all aspects of education there. In 1884 he was made an official (*Soninkan*) of the Imperial Household Agency which meant he was an official appointed by the Cabinet and reported on to the Emperor. At the age of twenty four it seems that he was beginning to be singled out as a possible high-flyer. In 1887 Kano was made acting director of the Gakushuin in the absence of the director.

In 1887 the son of Emperor Meiji came to the Gakushuin for education. His education was supervised by Lt. General Viscount Soga, but Kano was in charge of selecting his classmates and teachers and most likely taught his specialist subjects[31]. The boy later became Emperor Taisho in 1912 and ruled for fourteen years. One of the boy's teachers was Katsu Yasuyoshi (aka Kaishu the famous Zen kendo-ka and politician) and another by the name of Okano Keijiro who later became the Japanese Minister for Education. Some years before, Kaishu apparently taught the young Meiji Emperor kendo and on one occasion knocked him over. When the Court Chamberlain protested Kaishu shrugged and said 'if he wishes to learn kendo he must know what it is like to fall down'. Very few in Japan could have got away with that! Needless to say it was not long before Kano had set up a judo dojo in the Gakushuin.

The headship of the College changed a number of times while Kano was there but eventually a new man was brought in called Lieutenant-General Viscount Miura Goro who was a soldier-politician and former head of the Army College. Kano clashed with Miura but before that worked briefly as head of the College. The collision between the two led to Kano going his own way in 1889 but this period in the Gakushuin clarified his ideas about education and led to his eventual decision to devote himself to it. See also Chapter 13 under Kano the Educationalist for more on the Gakushuin.

It was not surprising that Kano decided to pursue education if one

---

[31] The teacher-student relationship can be a lifelong one in Japan!

considers the circumstances of the time. Japan had been rudely awakened from centuries of feudal slumber and was forced to modernise at breakneck speed. The Japanese had experienced aggression from Russian, American and British ships and had seen the fate of China at the hands of the colonial powers during the Opium Wars of 1842. There was a perceived external threat which had to be met by massive modernisation and this demanded education because there was much that they did not know. Japan rapidly imported foreign specialists of all kinds and sent its best young students abroad to gather knowledge.

One less obvious example of the difficulties the Japanese of the Meiji period encountered was the massive change in their language to accommodate the new ideas that were flowing in from the West. For example there was no word in Japanese for 'railway' and although the word could be written phonetically in imitation of the English using the *kana* alphabet it was a clumsy method (and still is today). So the Japanese turned to the Chinese who by virtue of not imposing centuries of isolation on themselves had become familiar with the new concepts earlier and created compound characters (two or more characters used together) to express foreign words. For example the Chinese used two characters – iron and road – to mean railway which in Japanese became *tetsu-do*, although the Chinese pronunciation would have been totally different. So Japan appropriated the Chinese vocabulary to express some Western ideas and objects, while turning its back generally on centuries of assimilated Chinese culture. A modern Japanese today would use very many words in speech that would have been totally unintelligible to their great-grandparents. Words written in the Japanese kana alphabet in imitation of a foreign word do not slot as easily into the language as former Chinese words written in characters[32].

The two watchwords of the time were *Bunmei Kaika* (the blossoming of civilisation) and Fukoku Kyohei (wealth and military strength)[33]. Yet curiously while Kano was vigorously pursuing the road of education he was also promoting jujitsu, demonstrating the Japanese ability to combine old and new.

[32] See Historical Grammar of Japanese by Sansom.
[33] Watchwords are a common Japanese method for summarising and implanting key ideas and policies.

Chapter 5
The Kodokan is Born in 1882

In 1882 Kano set up his dojo, which he called the Kodokan, and taught what he called Kodokan judo. As one would expect Kano started off with a very modest dojo and a handful of students. Slowly his dojo began to grow. From 1882 the Kodokan occupied a succession of dojos. It was not till 1906 that the dojo jumped to a respectable 300-mat size. Before that the dojos were quite small and the life of the dojo in any one place was rarely more than three years. In 1933 the Kodokan moved to the 500-mat Suidobashi dojo and then in 1958 it moved to the huge 1000-mat *Bunkyo* (*Kasuga-cho*) dojo creating an impressive centre of world judo.

It is common to date the Kodokan by the various dojos it inhabited. I have followed this method, especially with the earlier dojos, although there is overlap of eras with its organisational, technical and theoretical developments. See Appendix for a list of the dojos.

The Eisho-ji dojo
In February 1882 Kano decided to set up house, dojo and school in Tokyo and rented the library and an attached building in the grounds of the Eisho-ji temple in Shitaya ward, Kita-Inari-cho, and moved in[34]. Eisho-ji was a temple of the *Jodo* Buddhist (Pure Land) sect and its resident priest was a forty-six year old man by the name of Asahibo or Choshunbo depending on how you read the characters. In the attached building Kano installed his live-in students and took the two rooms of the library (one twelve and a half mat room and one seven mat room) as his study. Since this was quite spacious he made one of the rooms his judo dojo[35]. There he taught not only his live-in students but other day students and visitors.

[34] The ji of Eisho-ji means temple. Strictly speaking Kano established the Kodokan in the Eisho temple.

[35] Dojo means training hall. In a Buddhist temple the dojo is where the meditation or Sutra chanting takes place. This first dojo of Kano's was only 144 sq feet which at 12' x 12' would barely accommodate two randori couples.

Right from the start his Eisho-ji facility doubled as a school which he called the *Kano-juku* (*juku* = school) and a judo dojo called the Kodokan.. The dojo was of course for judo but at the juku he taught various subjects, quite informally to start with, but all centred on judo. Already at this point Kano had become convinced of the benefits of learning from physical experience (and not just from books or lectures) and gradually created a strict environment. It was not long before the school routine firmed up. Live-in students had to rise at 4.45am and retire at 9pm. On rising they had to clean the school inside and out and take it in turn to serve Kano's breakfast. Cakes were allowed once a month and no heating was permitted. Apart from breakfast, food was served only once a day and if they wanted to go outside the school permission had to be gained in advance. This harsh discipline was based on that of a *Ritsu*-Buddhist sect temple called Jomei-in in the Ueno area of Tokyo, which was run by a priest who was a student of Kano's grandfather.

Kano also carried on doing jujitsu there and asked Iikubo Tsunetoshi to come and teach kata and randori on a regular basis. This dojo combined several uses. When it was time for jujitsu the desks and writing materials were cleared away then put back after the training. The premises were used as a school, dojo, study, sleeping quarters and guest reception room, all within the precinct of the Buddhist temple. The founding of Kodokan Judo, to give it its full name, is generally reckoned to have been in 1882, but it would seem to have had mixed fortunes and functions in its first year or two and very few students. Curiously, there was a 50th anniversary celebration of the Kodokan on 23 November in 1934, which would date the founding of the Kodokan to 1884. This was closer to the date when the various Kodokan events and functions took shape.

At the Eisho-ji school and dojo the number of students was very small. In the first two years only twenty or so students joined the dojo. At the forefront of the newly enrolled students was Yamada Tsunejiro later called Tomita Tsunejiro 7th Dan. He was the father of Tomita Joyu who wrote the novel *Sugata Sanshiro*. Later in the same year Shida Shiro (later called Saigo Shiro 6th Dan) joined the Kodokan, and he was said to be the model for Sugata Sanshiro. Among the visiting students was Matsuoka a lecturer in physical education at the Gakushuin Peers School, Okeguchi who later became Viscount and a member of the House of Peers (*Kizoku-in*), Viscount Arima Sumibumi and Arima Sumiomi who was a high school lecturer. Also there were Viscount Yamaguchi Hirotatsu and many friends. Many of these early students would appear to be acquaintances and colleagues from the prestigious Tokyo Imperial University and the elite Gakushuin. Half of his students dropped out in the first couple of years. Kano the young jujitsu-ka and educationalist had yet to make his mark on the world.

Eisho-ji was not really suitable. Often the sound of break-falls startled the priest and worshippers at the temple. Occasionally the roof tiles slid down or the floor gave way, whereupon Kano would light a candle and Tomita Tsunejiro crept under the floor from the outside and repaired it. Right next door to the library was the main hall of the temple where the Buddhist mortuary tablets hung. They began to move from the impact of the training, so much so that the priest complained and the training in the library was stopped. A new twelve mat dojo was then constructed in an attached building. The size of the dojo jumped from roughly 4m x 4m to roughly 5m x 5m which was still quite small. Since a traditional Japanese room is constructed to lay 6' x 3' straw mats precisely in the space it easily doubles as a dojo or as residential accommodation.

The Kobunkan dojo

After only one year Kano moved his school and dojo with the help of businessman Murata Genzo, a friend of Kano's since the days when they both studied the Chinese classics together. Murata had set up the Nihon Kosan Company which carried out reclamation projects in Fukushima prefecture, but Murata needed an office in Tokyo and suggested to Kano that they share a house. They rented a house in Imagawakoji in the Kanda area of Tokyo in 1883. It was quite a big house and was suitable for Kano's live-in students but there was not a room suitable for a dojo. So Kano decided to make a dojo by refurbishing the clay storehouse of his nearby Kobunkan School. This was a school of literary education which he started in 1882 and which continued till 1889 when he made his long trip abroad to Europe. In the warehouse he laid ten straw mats equal to to about 4 x 4 metres.

The Kobunkan dojo continued for about six months but Kano had various problems with it. Kano had started his dojo with high ideals, but this was the period when his jujitsu was at its lowest ebb. Kano was just a young unknown teacher and it is safe to say that not many came to learn his judo. In fact half of the twenty or so registered students in the period 1882-84 dropped out.

Kano always tried to attend the training, but when other business prevented it he got Saigo Shiro to run the sessions. In summer when the weather was fine waiting for students to arrive was not so onerous but in winter waiting in the (unheated) dojo from 7am on Sundays was bitterly cold.

When Kano first started teaching he trained with Saigo, but at that time Saigo had not matured and he would get tired before Kano had warmed up, so Saigo would rest and then train again with him or work on technique.

Not only was the storehouse dojo small but there were various projections from the walls which they had to avoid banging against. Among the students were some strong ones who used their full power so Kano had to be careful how he led the training. Training in the Kobunkan dojo lasted only six months; Kano had to think about alternative premises.

As we have seen so far Kano started with the desire to prevent himself from being bullied at school and improve his physique generally. However he was already on the academic path at Tokyo University. This led him to jujitsu and the desire to improve his health and his next step was to a wider interest in education in general (especially physical education). Kano had already noted the poor health of many students which he thought could be improved through his judo.

He investigated other types of physical exercise often with his friend Motoyama, such as rowing, walking and hiking, baseball, gymnastics and athletics, but all, in his opinion, had various defects such as cost or accessibility, or were not as good as jujitsu for the physique. So he gradually came to the conclusion that a modified jujitsu was suited not only to the full development of the body but was also good for the temperament.

With regard to temperament Kano said of himself that formerly he got easily excited and tended to fly off the handle, but as he did more and more jujitsu he found that he got calmer, mentally stronger and more able to control himself. He also realised that the tactical and strategic principles of jujitsu could be applied to everyday life and that this use of the intelligence was an important type of intellectual training (chi-iku).

Why 'Kodokan' and 'judo'?

The words judo and jujitsu remained interchangeable for quite a long time in Japan after 1882. For example it was 'jujitsu' that became part of the national middle school physical education curriculum in 1911 despite the fact that it was actually Kano's Kodokan Judo. However Kano did not adopt the old name of jujitsu to describe what he taught but significantly used the word judo. Kano explained why as follows:

'At the time a few *bujitsu* (martial arts) experts still existed but bujitsu was almost abandoned by the nation at large. Even if I wanted to teach jujitsu most people had now stopped thinking about it. So I thought it better to teach under a different name principally because my objectives were much wider than jujitsu. I wanted to stop using the word jujitsu but since what I taught was based on what I had been taught by my jujitsu teachers I thought it pointless to drop the word altogether. So I kept the single character *ju*, meaning soft or compliant, in the name and called my art ju-do meaning the Compliant Way. However the word judo was not new – it had been used by the *Jikishin* jujitsu school of Izumo province. Nevertheless the use of this word was very rare – most people in Japan used the word *Jujitsu, Yawara* or *Tai-jitsu*. For that reason it is safe to say that I started the use of the word judo. The word Kendo barely existed in the past so the modern use of the word Kendo (the Way of the sword) is probably because of the example set by judo. The use of this suffix *-do* is quite different to its use in the word *Ka-do* (the Way of Flower Arranging) for example. Judo follows a more fundamental Way. Nowadays most people do not use the word Kodokan judo but use the word judo on its own. Compared with jujitsu, the judo I teach is a whole dimension different.

Because of my use of the name ju **do**, I named the place where I taught it the *Ko-do-kan* (literally Expounding the Way Building). This was because I wanted to make clear that I did not simply teach the martial arts. If I wanted to name a place where the martial arts were taught I would have called it *Ko-bu-kan* (the bu meaning martial). The reason I avoided that was because I wanted to make clear that my Way (*do*) was more fundamental and the techniques were the application of that Way. Thus in February 1882 I founded the Kodokan and the Kano-juku (The Kano School) in the precinct of Eisho-ji.'

The Five Article Oath (Gokajo no Seimon)

The establishment of the Oath and Students' Register were the first official functions of the new Kodokan. The Oath was solemnly pledged by all those who began training at the Kodokan. Somewhat dramatically it was signed and sealed in blood. It headed the Students' Register which came into effect in 1882 and read as follows:

1. Having entered the Kodokan I request instruction and training in judo and will not cease my study of it
2. I will do nothing to sully the honour of the dojo
3. I will not tell the secrets of judo to others or show them without permission
4. I will not teach without permission
5. I will strictly adhere to the various rules of the Kodokan and after I have qualified I will continue to observe the rules even when I am engaged in teaching

The registration of new members under the oath was pursued from when the Kodokan was first established in 1882. However in 1884 the names of those who had stopped training were eliminated from the register, leaving only nine people who were still training. They included Tomita Tsunejiro, Saigo Shiro and Kawai Keijiro. This somewhat reinforces the view that the Kodokan only began to take shape from about 1884. However, Kano had begun to gather judo-ka of substance around him.

The fact that Kano came up with five oaths for Kodokan new entrants was significant because in 1868, with the accession of the new Meiji Emperor, a Charter Oath was promulgated in which the aims of the new government were laid down. This too consisted of five oaths and was also known as the Go-kajo no Seimon. Article four stated that uncivilised customs of former times were to be discontinued and all new customs should be based upon just and equitable principles of nature. Article five ordered that knowledge should be sought throughout the world. Most adult Japanese would have been familiar with the Meiji Charter Oath and would have understood Kano's ambitions to modernise jujitsu.

Chapter 6
The Early Flowering of the Kodokan
1883-1886

The 1st Kami-niban-cho Era (1883-86)

After only six months in the Kobunkan dojo Kano began looking for other more suitable premises. In 1883 Kano rented a house in Kami-niban-cho in Kojimachi ward, Tokyo. This house belonged to a Shinto priest and consisted of seven to eight rooms. Next to the entrance was an eight mat room which he used as a dojo. The other rooms accommodated his library, study and students. Even though his judo students were few the eight mat dojo was too small, so it was enlarged by demolishing two cupboards which added another two mats of space. Thereafter his student numbers began to increase, but the training soon began to suffer as a consequence so an outside space was used to build a 20 mat dojo (equal to roughly 6m x 6m).

At that time Kano was a lecturer at the Gakushuin (Peers College) and Komaba Agricultural University, which kept him busy. When his work finished he hurried to his dojo, changed into his judo suit (*gi*) and if it was cold he put a kimono on over it and read in his dojo till students arrived. When they did arrive the desks were tidied away and training began. During this period Kano ploughed relentlessly on with his studies, his jujitsu and his judo. In October 1883 Kano received his *Kito-ryu* licence (*menkyo*) from Iikubo and all the documentation that related to it.

One story illustrates the mood of the time. Around 1885 two foreign brothers came to train at the dojo. One was very large and weighed about eighty kilos which was considerably larger than most Japanese. Saigo however handled him like a baby which stirred up considerable interest and increased the reputation of the dojo. This was a somewhat jingoistic time (Japan was warring with China) and pitching big foreigners around drew the crowds. Otake of the Totsuka Yoshin-ryu also came to make a challenge but Saigo threw him all over the place. Many others began to challenge the Kodokan about this time.

The Kuzushi revelation

Just before receiving the Kito-ryu licence Kano had a technical revelation that greatly affected the future development of judo. Kano, while running his dojo and school, had carried on learning kata and randori from Iikubo. Iikubo was 48 years old at the time and still very strong. In randori he was much better than Kano. But one day when Kano was doing randori with this Kito-ryu teacher his throws began to work well. Hitherto he had been able to throw him occasionally but mostly it was Iikubo who did the throwing. That day it was different from before – he was not thrown even once by Iikubo and Kano's techniques worked well. Kano thought this strange and pondered on it, then realised his study of balance-breaking (*kuzushi*) was bearing fruit. In the early days the kuzushi was in six directions but later on it expanded to the present eight-direction kuzushi.

Kano talked about this to Iikubo who said, 'You've got it. You do not have to learn much more than this. Carry on training with the young ones and deepen your studies of this principle'. After that Iikubo stopped doing free-fighting with Kano. Even so Kano kept on studying kata with him. Iikubo worked for the state postal services and regularly dropped in the dojo to teach on his way back from work. In 1888 he died aged 53.

In his book, *Judo Kyohon*, Kano explained his Kuzushi principle in more detail:

'Tsukuri is where one destabilizes (kuzushi) the opponent's body and puts one's own body in the right position (shintai o kamaeru) in order to facilitate the throw and *kake* is the completing of the technique (waza o hodokosu) on the destabilized body. When doing standing randori it is best to concentrate on tsukuri in the beginning and then later on practise putting power into the finish of it. This is because there is the danger of injury to the opponent if he is not so strong.'

So *tsukuri* (which includes kuzushi) seems to be the setting up of the throw including the positioning of the thrower and *kake* is finishing it off.

Kuzushi comes from the verb *kuzusu* meaning to break or crush but it has other slightly different meanings for example to deregulate something or simplify a Japanese character or change the rhythmn or mood (of Noh drama etc). Kinko o yaburu is the modern verb for breaking balance. Perhaps destabilize might be a good translation of kuzushi. Be that as it may the illustrations of kuzushi in the book clearly show the breaking of balance in eight directions.

Kuzushi is a subtle concept. One *sensei* I went to Japan stressed the need for light kuzushi. Do not always do it strongly he would often say, it will work against you. In Judo Kyohon kuzushi is clearly shown as part of the preparation for a throw which includes the attacker moving his body into position at the same time. However the opening eight-path kuzushi and the final direction the opponent is thrown are not always the same[36]. Kuzushi is also not so applicable when the opponent is moving freely. It seems more applicable against a static position. Later Kodokan technical explanations describe kuzushi as an *offensive* principle as opposed to the higher *defensive* compliancy principle of Ju.

The Kodokan kata

Kano in his early jujitsu and judo days practised kata from both the Tenjinshinyo and Kito jujitsu styles and went on to create his own kata. Kano said that he thought of kata as the grammar of judo. A person can write or talk ungrammatically and communicate to a degree, he said, but to communicate fully, the grammar and syntax of the sentence must be correct. Kano likened kata (choreographed/arranged sequences) and randori (free fighting) to this concept of communication and grammar and placed great emphasis on both in judo training. In the first five years of the Kodokan to 1887, Kano laid down the six basic kata; the Nage no Kata, Katame no Kata, Ju no Kata, Kime no Kata, Koshiki no kata[37] and Itsutsu no Kata. With regard to kata and randori he explained:

'Through the jujitsu kata one learns to handle defences and attacks from many directions but perfecting them is difficult. However studying kata in fixed sequences means that if somebody comes at you from an unusual angle this will cause panic and injury may occur. Consequently it is very necessary to compete in a situation where you do not know how the opponent will come at you or what he will do, as in randori. When randori is practised in this way along with the kata it becomes a complete training.

[36] In sacrifice throws (sutemi waza) for example.

[37] Kano did not create this kata. It was a Kito-ryu kata which he retained.

So I researched and thought about both kata and randori. As a result I noted that against a person with a little bit of randori training the old kata training did not have much effect and that randori was more realistic than kata and consequently more interesting. I began to fear that kata would be ignored so in the early days of the Kodokan I did not teach the kata separately from the randori. I adopted the principle of teaching the kata in between the randori and weaving them together. This was like mixing grammar and composition at the same time. In the early days I was able to do this myself without any problems but when the numbers grew I found it took too much time to teach this individually to the students and had to operate a system of alternate training (kawari-geiko). I came to realise that my initial method was difficult to execute. I felt the need to lay down new kata'.

Sakko Vol 6, No 12. 1927

In the beginning Kano taught the Kito-ryu and Tenjinshinyo-ryu jujitsu kata in their original form. Depending on the content and degree of his students' ability he then awarded the *Menjo* (diploma) to them. It is recorded that he awarded the Tenjinshinyo-ryu diploma to Mizukuri Ganpachi and the Kito-ryu diploma to Tomita Tsunejiro. Each of these jujitsu kata had their strong points, but since they were constructed according to different systems Kano felt the need to create new kata according to his own ideas. With this in mind he first created his Nage no Kata (the kata of throwing) about 1884-86. Kano said about this:

'I began by creating the Nage no Kata which at first consisted of ten techniques then fifteen which it still is. As for differences between the two, only the present *Kata-guruma* and *Sumi-gaeshi* throws are different from the early kata.

When I am asked why I created the new kata I replied that formerly I taught technique with randori but with the great increase in student numbers I could not do that so I chose three comparatively workable representative techniques from the hand, hip and leg throws and three from the straight sacrifice and side sacrifice techniques to create the Nage no Kata. Using this kata I tried to impart the understanding of the principles of throwing'.

Sakko Vol 6, No 12. 1927

The second kata that was created was the Katame no Kata (the kata of groundwork). Representative techniques were chosen from *osaekomi-waza* (restraints), *shime-waza* (strangles) and *kansetsu waza* (joint-locks) to illustrate the principles of groundwork. To start with the kata consisted of ten techniques in total. This was later increased to fifteen in 1906.

Then sometime later the *Shinken Shobu no Kata* (real combat kata) was created. This was later called the *Kime no Kata*. The first two kata (Nage and Katame no Kata) were for teaching the principles of randori (free-fighting)and were collectively called the randori kata but the Shinken Shobu no kata was created for actual combat and drew upon the kata of various jujitsu schools, plus some other ideas of Kano. This kata at first consisted of fifteen techniques but was later increased to twenty techniques when the Dai-Nippon Butokukai recognised it (see Chapter 9 under the Establishment of the Butokukai Kata).

Kano said about the Kime no Kata:

'This kata emerged somewhat later than the two Randori Kata and was only 15 techniques at first. The objective of the Kime no Kata was the same as the old jujitsu kata of the various schools[38]. Namely it was a kata of real combat. I may be generalising but when I look at the old kata as practised at present there are not a few points that make me wonder if they had not forgotten the spirit of the time when they were first established. I often felt that many of them would not work against somebody who had trained a bit in free-fighting. For that reason whichever jujitsu kata I looked at I felt dissatisfied so I took the essence from those kata, added my own ideas and what you now see is the former Shinken Shobu no Kata or the present Kime no Kata'.

Sakko Vol 6, No. 12

The next katas, which were composed about 1887 were the *Ju no kata*, *Go no kata* and the *Itsutsu no kata*. The *Ju no kata* which has various unique points was first called the *Taiso no kata* (the kata of exercise). Its first main point is that it teaches the principle *Ju Yoku Go Seisuru* (the yielding overcomes the resistant) so when one side pushes the other side retreats, and when one side tries to pull the other side lets itself be pulled and uses

[38] Kime means decisive techniques, in other words techniques that finish the fight.

it to unbalance the other. Through the practice of this kata correct advancing and retreating methods are practised. The second feature of the Ju no kata is that while randori tends to be rough the gentle principles of the Ju no kata can be understood while gently exercising the body. The third feature of Ju no Kata is that the throws are not completed, so the moves can be done on hard ground, in a cramped space or without a judogi by male or female, young and old. And the techniques of real combat can be learned at the same time. At first this kata consisted of ten techniques but in 1907 the number was increased to the present 15 techniques.

The *Go no kata* (or the Kata of Resistance) was constructed in contrast to the *Ju no kata*. It starts with strength used against strength but then turns to yielding methods and wins. Not much is known about this kata, which did not survive long.

The *Itsutsu no kata* (the Kata of Five) consists of only five moves. The first two moves show technical principles and the last three moves skilfully portray in the movements of the human body the movement of water, the movement of the heavenly bodies and the myriad movements of the universe.

The *Koshiki no kata* (the old-style kata) is a kata of the Kito-ryu style of jujitsu which Kano kept in his new system, perhaps for nostalgic reasons as it was a fine example of an old-style jujitsu kata. It is sometimes referred to as the *Kito no kata*.

It is often difficult to explain to non-judo people what a judo kata really is. As explained above they have different functions, but when seen for the first time they look rather slow and posed and sometimes out of date. They have to be learned in a very precise way. Every movement is laid down and there is no room for improvisation. Japanese teachers often bicker over the minutest points[39]. Although they are one of judo's training methods they have tended over the years to be used as formal demonstrations of judo techniques and are often performed at judo events. Indeed one dictionary definition of Kata is *form*. The root of the word is *katai* meaning hard and indicates something that has hardened into shape.

[39] I was once asked by the Kodokan to demonstrate the Nage no Kata in Sendai with George Kerr. Before going there we had to perform the Kata endlessly in front of the Kodokan teachers who could not always agree on the minute details.

Japan is often said to be a formal society where there are specific ways of doing nearly everything. The concept of kata is obviously important to the Japanese. There is also an element of Japanese theatre about them. Japanese Noh and Kabuki drama feature similarly slow, stylized movements and posturing. Kata is often translated as formal demonstrations of judo.

Kano incorporated kata and randori into his system but he was innovative in many ways. There is one account during this time which gives a very good idea of Kano's innovative approach to the teaching of judo. He ordered a craftsman to make 20cm high wooden dolls, able to move freely in the joints, and used them to explain to students how to make kuzushi and apply technique.

Annual events and functions

A dojo for Kano was not simply a matter of providing mat space, judo kits, instruction and free-fighting. From about 1884 Kano introduced various annual events and functions into the Kodokan that helped consolidate it, add value and set it on course for expansion. Some of the functions were based on traditional Japanese annual events such as the New Year's Day Ceremony (*Gantan-shiki*) but others were new expressions of Kano's ideals.

New Year's Day Ceremony (*Gantan-shiki*)

The judo year started with the New Year's Day ceremony (*Gantan-shiki*). It was celebrated by the live-in Kano-juku students who got up before daybreak to clean the premises and then sipped *toso* (spiced *sake*) to welcome in the New Year. Kano created a particular ceremony for this which gives an interesting insight into his educational ideals:

'I think this happened from about 1884. At first I as head of the school poured some *toso* into a cup, then without drinking a drop of it passed it on to the next senior member who also poured in a little *toso* in his cup and then in turn passed it on to the other students. When it had been passed round to everybody it ended up with me again. The first round consisted of pouring *toso* into the cup but not drinking a drop of it. In the next round the toso cup was passed around but nothing was poured in nor drunk. The third time the cup was passed around I sipped some *toso* but less than I had first poured in and so on till it had been passed to everybody, leaving some *toso* left over. This was not drunk and the cup was stored away.

The significance of the ceremony was as follows. The pouring in of the *toso* in the first round signified one's work or what one had put into the school. The next round when the *toso* was not drunk expressed the spirit of deferment to others. The third round signified taking less out of our enterprise than we had put in. That which was left over became our common capital and was saved. Later on the numbers of students increased so that the second round had to be omitted and two cups were used; one was passed from the right and the other from the left both at the same time, and eventually both ended up in my hands.

This ceremony helped foster the Kano-juku custom of overcoming difficulties, overcoming the self, working hard and studying hard and gracefully setting aside one's achievements and rank for the sake of others'.

Mirror opening ceremony (*Kagamibiraki-shiki*)

This Kodokan annual event known as the *Kagamibiraki-shiki* (literally Mirror Opening Ceremony) began about 1884. Originally the *Kagamibiraki* was a Japanese festival held in samurai households on the 20th of January which was later shifted to the 11th of January. On this day the sons were presented with sword accoutrements and the daughters with a mirror stand. All then ate *kagami-mochi* (round mirror-shaped rice cake).

At the Kodokan a modified Kagamibiraki-shiki was held on the second Sunday of January after the morning's *Kangeiko* (mid-winter practice). In the first part of the ceremony Kano gave a talk about judo, representatives of the members exchanged greetings and then kata and randori were demonstrated. After that various awards were given for achievements in the past year – selected from among all sections of the Kodokan from high to low. The ceremony finished at 11.30am and then the Kagami-mochi, which was brought by the Tokyo residents among the membership, was made into a red bean soup with rice cake or turned into *Age-mochi* and given to all present. Those who had been promoted to Dan grade on that day served as hosts, waited on the guests and looked after everybody. New Dan grades usually attended the Kagami-biraki ceremony. As the Kodokan grew in size and strength there came a point in 1930 when the Kagami-biraki was held in the Hibiya Public Hall and was open to the general public.

The Red and White contests and the Monthly Contests

According to the Kodokan Judo Yearbook (*Kodokan Nenkan*) both the *Kohaku-shobu* (red and white team contests) and the *Tsuki-nami shobu* (monthly contests) began in 1884. However, Kano said that competition was encouraged before that and that both types of *shobu* – later called *shiai* – began about 1885. The format of the competitions took a while to firm up so this discrepancy in dates probably reflects that process.

The monthly contest was fought once a month on a Sunday. It started with the weakest one taking on the next strongest and whoever won the match stayed on and took on the next in the line. The placing of the competitors was decided in advance based on their respective strengths and grades, as shown in previous contests. This method was good when the numbers were low but became more problematic when the numbers increased. However the name of the competition and the basic method survives to this day in the Kodokan. Presently the monthly contest is fought by black belts up to and including 3rd dan grade, and points gained in the system go towards promotion, which also includes a kata test. Those who get an excellent result (*batsugun*) such as beating six people in a row qualify for instant promotion subject to passing the Kata test.

The Red and White contest was divided into two teams (red and white) beforehand and was fought on the basis of winner stays on. Each team was originally divided according to age, grade and ability with all participating from the lowest to the highest. It survives to this day and is fought twice a year, in spring and autumn. In these competitions 4th Dan and above can also participate and wins gained go towards promotion[40]. Kata is also tested separately once there are sufficient wins. The *Batsugun* rule also applies here.

Both these competitions were held to encourage the participants and in the early days of the Kaminiban-cho era they usually finished before noon. However around the time of the First World War there was a big increase in new students into the Kodokan and the Kohaku-shobu had to

---

[40] In my first Kohaku shiai as a 4th dan I fought two 4th dans. The first one I threw with Uchimata and drew with the second. I was much relieved to win my first 4th dan fight.

be held over two days. Then from 1916 it increased to three days, which included one day for non-Dan grades.

Mid-winter training (*Kangeiko*)

Both this cold winter training and the *Shochugeiko* (hot summer training) which started much later in 1896 were devised to strengthen the spirit of the trainees. During the coldest and hottest times of the year the students gathered to train without heating or air conditioning of any kind. It still survives in the Kodokan today. Those who successfully complete each training period, which are a month long, are awarded a certificate at the end.

Promotion Ceremony (*Shokyu-shodan-shiki*)

In the early days when numbers were small, promotion certificates within the Kyu and Dan grades were handed out at the Shodan-Shokyu-Shiki (Promotion ceremonies). When numbers grew rapidly this ceremony became a bit of a problem and tended to be preserved in representative form at the annual Gantan-shiki or Kagamibiraki-shiki.

The Dan and Kyu ranking system

One of the features of Kodokan judo is the coloured belt worn round the middle to show rank and ability. Once achieved the grade is never lost. Jujitsu, the forerunner of judo, had ranks but these were not shown by coloured belts. In the early Japanese martial arts proficiency was usually shown in the *Inka* (permission) and *Menkyo* (licence) system but not exclusively so. For example at the end of the Tokugawa period one feudal clan used a simple *Dan* system for all the martial arts in its clan school. This was at three levels.

Although Dan and Kyu mean virtually the same thing in Japanese, in the Kodokan system the Dan grades are the more advanced ones. The use of such a Dan grade system in Japan first appeared in the board game known as *Igo* or *Go* and dates back to the early Tokugawa period (from about 1600)[41]. The system survives to the present day in both *Igo* and *Shogi* (Japanese chess) etc. Other Japanese arts later adopted Dan ranking systems but many did not go beyond 8th Dan.

[41] An old Japanese and Chinese board game of territorial possession and capture.

It is not clear by what process Kano arrived at the use of the Dan system and what the justification is for fifteen grades (if the Kyu ones are added in). However the system goes back at least to 1883 when Tomita Tsunejiro and Saigo Shiro were the first to be listed as *Shodan* (1st Dan). It is probably safe to say that rank has always been important in China and Confucian Japan hence its widespread use there.

One separate innovation was the use of the black belt to show the Dan grade. The black belt quickly became the desire of all trainees. Although the Dan system existed from 1883, it was about another three years before that rank was shown by the black belt. Before that it did not exist in judo or in the other jujitsu styles. It was probably the invention of Kano. It is said that when the Kodokan team appeared wearing their white judo-gi and black belts at the Keishicho Bujitsu Taikai (Tokyo Police Martial Arts Championships) they stood out conspicuously against the other jujitsu-ka who were wearing the traditional kimono garb of hakama and haori.

New judo students were called Hosshin-sha to start with and wore a light blue belt[42]. Once they began to go up the ranks they then became Mu-dansha (non-dan grades) and were ranked 5th Kyu to 1st Kyu in ascending order. However there were separate colour belts for youths and adults. Youths of grades 3rd – 1st Kyu wore purple belts and adults of the same grade wore brown belts. Youths and adults of 5th to 4th Kyu wore white belts.

Having reached 1st Kyu the next step was to move into the Dan grades, known collectively as Yudan-sha. Until 1932 all Dan grades wore a black belt. In 1932 the system changed so that 1st to 5th Dans wore a black belt, 6th to 9th Dans wore a red and white belt and 10th Dans wore a red belt of the same size and thickeness of the other Dan grade belts. However 6th Dans and above were allowed to wear black belts if they wished but were expected to wear their red or red and white belts for formal occasions.

For comparison, rank in sumo is shown by position on the Banzuke or ranking list which is purely based on results in the most recent Basho or tournaments (like pro-tennis). They do, however, take with them into retirement the highest rank they achieved. Pro-sumo allows its wrestlers

---

[42] Hosshin-sha means one who has experienced religious awakening. Here it is used in the sense of realizing that here is a worthwhile Way to follow and beginning the training.

to wear whichever colour belt they like but the colour black is often used by some of the top rikishi such as Yokozuna Asashoryu because it 'imparts a sense of authority and power.' Amateur sumo in Japan has Dan ranks denoted by black sumo belts. See also Chapter 9 – The Butokukai Ranking System and Chapter 10 – The Kyu and Dan Grade System.

Judo and money

When Kano first opened the *Eisho*-ji dojo no fee was payable either for the instruction or for the dojo training. With regard to this Kano said:

> 'At that time I was searching widely for trainees and decided to charge no fees for instruction or dojo use. This was because I was more influenced by old Japanese ideas than Western ones. In other words I believed that teaching the Way to people was not something that should be charged for. However when new students first joined the Kodokan there was a rule that they should present a fan to the dojo.'

From its foundation the Kodokan was supported by Kano, who even went as far as providing judo suits for new students. From 1894 however a modest fee of 1 yen was levied as a joining fee for new students, and again in 1904 a 10 sen levy per month was introduced to cover running costs[43]. With regard to this entrance fee Kano wrote that his objective was not only to collect money but to prevent the many 'rubbernecks' who got in the way of those who really wanted to study his judo. Kano also made clear that no money should ever be charged for tuition. With regard to teachers of judo who had no other means of making a living, Kano believed that they should be paid modestly for teaching[44]. Kano compared judo to religions such as Christianity and Buddhism which do not charge students to learn their teachings. 'What the founders of these religions did was not done to gain reward; consequently they did not have to think about the balance between reward and work. It was natural that such people (those who taught for reward) would want to work as little as possible for the greatest reward. Education is not the same as religion but there are many similarities', said Kano.

---

[43] A sen is one hundreth of a yen.
[44] Cf. Vol. 3 of Kano Chosaku-shu.

The author notes: When I trained at the Kodokan between 1960 and 1964 I was charged nothing. Later on I heard that foreigners were charged a monthly amount although this might have been for those who only trained in the International (*Kokusai*) Dojo where instruction was plenty and the training was not as hard as the main dojo. It seemed the main source of the Kodokan's income came from grading fees and certificates. Japanese who attain black belt, for example, have to pay the registration and certification charges which increase the higher they climb. This is perhaps the reason why the Kodokan fought so hard over the right to award grades.

When karate first appeared in the UK it charged much more than judo. Attempts were made to raise the judo fees to the karate level but this was resisted. There was a definite feeling that judo should be cheap and this probably came from Koizumi of the Budokwai, who was probably influenced by Kano. At the time I wondered if cheap fees had a religious base.

As can be seen the basic structure of the Kodokan was set up in the two years from 1884 to 1886 – in the 1st Kami-niban-cho era. The number of students was not large but many of the later famous students joined during this period.

Among the famous students of the Kami-niban-cho era were Yuasa Takejiro who made a name for himself as commander of the *Sagami-maru* in the blockade of Port Arthur (Lushun in China), English literature scholar Honda Masujiro, Munakata Itsuro who later instructed at the Kodokan, Seki Juichiro head of the Kodokan office, Yamashita Yoshiaki the first man to grade 10th Dan and Nango Jiro who later became the second head of the Kodokan.

Chapter 7
From Fits and Starts to Critical Mass
1886-1906

This period spans twenty years, during which time the Kodokan leapt in size. It was a time when Kano's growing work commitments and career interfered somewhat with his judo, but he managed to keep his fledgling dojo on track.

The Fujimi-cho Era (1886 - 1889)

In 1886 Viscount Shinagawa Shojiro was appointed Japanese Ambassador to Germany. He did not want to rent out his Fujimi-cho house in Tokyo while he was away and asked Kano if he would house-sit for him. The connection between Kano and Shinagawa was through Murata Genzo who was both friend and student of Kano. Murata was a native of Yamaguchi prefecture and with the patronage of Shinagawa and others was helped with his expenses when studying in America. Kano helped organise this and got to know Shinagawa, who developed a considerable understanding of Kano's judo and his educational philosophy and was well disposed towards him. At one point during the second election of the House of Representatives it is recorded that Kano went to Saga in order to protect Viscount Shinagawa who was in some danger due to the virulent politics of the time. The two remained life-long good friends.

The Viscount's house in Fujimi-cho occupied one thousand *tsubo* of land (3300sq metres) of which over 100 tsubo (330sqm) had Western and Japanese style buildings on it. Kano at the time was living a bachelor existence in his seven-room house along with his students and employed an older woman who helped with the cooking. Kano worried that his students might damage the Viscount's house, which was too grand anyway, and declined the offer. The Viscount replied saying he did not mind that at all and he did not need the rent either, and suggested that Kano paid the same amount of rent he currently paid and move into his place. He pressed Kano to accept this offer and eventually Kano agreed.

In 1886 he moved into Viscount Shinagawa's house along with his students, and a 40-mat dojo of roughly 9m x 9m was constructed on a plot in the estate. From 1886 until 1889 when Kano went abroad on a long fact-finding trip this period is known as the Fujimi-cho era of the Kodokan. It was a most active and productive period for Kano and judo. According to the records, by 1886 he had signed up 98 students but within three years of moving to Fujimi-cho this had climbed to 605 students! No doubt the grandness of the dojo and its location added to his mission.

Among those who attended as judo specialist students were Saigo Shiro, Yamashita Yoshiaki, Yokoyama Sakujiro, Tobari Takisaburo, Sato Hoken and Kimotsuke Munetsugi. Among the hard-training non-specialists were Munakata Itsuro, Honda Masujiro, Yuasa Takejiro, Tamura Katsukazu, Oda Katsutaro, Kano Tokusaburo, Oshima Hidenotsuke/eijo, Hirose Takeo and Kawai Keijiro.

Patriotic fervour

The patriotic fervour that sprang from the successful Sino-Japanese war of 1894-95 and the later Russo-Japanese war of 1904-1905 visibly swelled the ranks of the Kodokan and led to a big increase in judo competitions up and down the country[45]. Sumo also benefited from it and was able to build a magnificent new centre in Ryogoku called the Kokugikan. However, there seems little evidence that the few surviving jujitsu schools such as the Yoshin-ryu benefited from this fervour. The reason for this may have been that it was only Kano who caught the mood of the time, which was pro-modernisation.

Kano recognised that jujitsu had strong and weak points and could be adapted. So he changed the name (rebranding it), described judo as a form of physical education, which was a relatively newly imported Western concept, but gave it values that merged with the Imperial Rescript on Education and its concepts of moral education (*toku-iku*) and intellectual education (*chi-iku*)[46]. He also had a rather splendid dojo in Fujimi-cho.

[45] Some might say Jingoism

[46] Meiji period Japanese physical education was generally divided into Swedish exercises, German exercises and English competitive exercises (kyogi undo). Kyogi undo was their word for sport but later on the English word 'sportsu' was used. It has been claimed that Japanese does not have a word for sport but 'competitive exercise' describes it well enough I think.

Kano was not only a moderately wealthy educationalist but also a bureaucrat. In 1884 he was made *Soninkan* (an official appointed with Imperial approval) and in 1916 he was made Senior Official 1st Class (*Kotokan Itto*). He had good connections and was well able to plot the course of the Kodokan through difficult bureaucratic waters. For example in 1896 the Ministry of Education ordered an enquiry by the School Hygiene Advisory Council into the hygenic pluses and minuses of jujitsu and gekken. There was no way that judo would pop up unprepared and unannounced in the school curriculum and it needed someone like Kano to negotiate its progress.

Most importantly, he devised a set of free–fighting rules very early on which clicked right away. It was not long before his students realised how good his judo was for competitive exercise. In the process he planted the seed of Asia's first Olympic 'sport.'

There was one other factor and that was Japan's latent pride in its past and its traditions. The forced opening of the country by the USA and others was a big blow to Japan's pride. Successes in wars against China and Russia helped salve that, so while the volatile mood of the country was currently for 'Westernisation', underneath lurked the belief that Japan was best. Abandoning jujitsu was not the way ahead nor was resurrecting the old jujitsu – modernising it was.

Kano's career development and the *Tokyo Koto Shihan Gakko*

This period also marked a crucial formative stage in Kano's academic life. Kano had entered the new Tokyo Imperial University in 1878, then graduated in 1882 (including an extra year for the Philosophy course) but in the same year he became a lecturer at the Gakushuin (Peers College) where he continued to teach till 1889. This put him in direct contact with the highest in the land although it seems the Imperial connection via the Shogenji family was there long before. Then after a brief interlude in the provinces he was appointed head of Japan's only male teacher training institute – the Tokyo Koto Shihan Gakko. In the short space of ten years he worked or studied in key Japanese educational institutions.

By the age of twenty-eight he had already firmed up his strong ideas on education and physical education in particular. In 1888 we see him making an early lecture on Kodokan Judo to the Japanese Education Society (see Chapter 11 – The Japanese Education Society Lecture) where he made a powerful case for judo's physical, mental and moral educational values. In the process he steered a steady path between the old and the new and matched it to the Imperial Rescript on Education.

Jujitsu versus judo (Kodokan judo versus Yoshin-ryu Jujitsu)

One event during this period on which many words have been written was a match between the newly emerging Kodokan and the Totsuka based Yoshin-ryu jujitsu school. The Kodokan later claimed it as a great victory but there are few facts to support the claim either way. Kano himself wrote that during the period of the Sino-Japanese war of 1894-5 when patriotic fervour swept the country, membership of the Kodokan rapidly swelled and many jujitsu-ka came visiting to challenge the new 'jujitsu' school in the old tradition of dojo-yaburi (dojo breaking). This, it seems, was when some of the jujitsu masters such as Tanabe Mataemon of the Fusen-ryu gave the Kodokan men a hard time on the ground. However, the big match between the Kodokan and the Totsuka Yoshin jujitsu school was supposedly in 1885 at the first Tokyo Metropolitan Police Martial Arts Championships (Keishicho Bujitsu Taikai).

The Keishicho began hosting competitions and demonstrations of the martial arts both by its own policemen and other invited experts and masters from 1885. Its purpose was to encourage these arts, particularly gekken and jujitsu, and the creation of fighting spirit (*shiki*). The Kodokan, which had begun to attract attention because of the scholar who had started judo, was also invited, and the chance arrived to compare its strength against the strongest jujitsu school, the Totsuka–Yoshin-ryu[47].

Little is known about this event except for a few snippets, mainly from the Kodokan side. There seems to be no authoritative account by independent sources. One cause of the present confusion is the mixture of fact and fiction that resulted from a number of Japanese novels and movies on judo which mention the match. For example there was the novel *Sugata Sanshiro* (the fictional hero) which was based on the exploits of *Saigo Shiro* of the Kodokan.

Among the references that exist are the following: 'In the Keishicho Bujitsu Championships held in May 1885 a bout was held between Saigo

---

[47] The fact that an academic from the merchant and priest classes had created his own successful 'jujitsu' school would have been a newsworthy event.

Shiro of the Kodokan and Terashima of the Yoshin-ryu. In this bout Saigo hurled Terashima with his special left *Yama-arashi* throw and won the match. This marked the first big step in the recognition of the Kodokan'.

Note that Saigo won this with a big-throw and not with a small throw which predominated, as later Kodokan accounts claimed.

Tomita Tsunejiro wrote as follows: 'It was May 1885. The place was the Tokyo Met Police Office in Marunouchi. The rivals were Terashima Taro, the top student of famous Chiba-based Yoshin-ryu master Totsuka Hikokuro. Terashima was already a famous fighter but Saigo Shiro was still an unknown youngster of the Kano dojo'[48].

Isogai Hajime 10th Dan, who joined the Kodokan in 1891, also wrote,

'In 1885 there was a match in the Keishicho between the Kodokan and the Totsuka-ryu. At the time the Keishicho had decided to invite teachers from the Kodokan to help with the training of the police, but among them there was a division between those who said the already famous Totsuka wing of the Yoshin-ryu school should be invited and those who preferred the newly arisen and vigorous Kodokan. It was decided to have a match between the two to see which was the stronger. Each side fielded ten men. The result was one draw and nine wins to the Kodokan.

As for how the individual matches were won the small throws such as *Ashi-harai, Ko-uchi-gari, Hiza-guruma, O-uchi-gari,* and small counter techniques were mostly used. It was the small techniques and the nimble body movements (*tai-sabaki*) of the Kodokan that overwhelmed the famed Osoto-gari throw and groundwork of the Totsuka wing of the Yoshin-ryu.[49]'

In the Yomiuri newspaper of May the 8th 1885 there is a reference to one Sugimura who was a member of the police Batto-tai (sword unit), which was successfully employed by the government in the Seinan revolt. He attended a big fencing competition (*Dai Gekken-kai*) at the Keishicho HQ at Danjibashi where he had a couple of bouts. He took ill after returning home and died shortly after. It is thought that this Keishicho-hosted event

---

[48] See Judo. Vol 2-6. (Yama-arashi and Saigo).
[49] "Genyaku Jidai (My Training Years). Judo Zasshi 1941"

may well have been the Keishicho Bujitsu Taikai mentioned above and confirms the dates mentioned earlier by Tomita and Isogai.

However Kano himself talked about the event as follows:

'In the Fujimicho period the number of those who came from all over to challenge the Kodokan increased as the fame of the Kodokan grew. There are some noteworthy facts relating to the match held at the Keishicho, namely the match against the students of the Totsuka dojo of the Yoshin-ryu. Among the jujitsu-ka of the late Tokugawa period the one with the strongest students was Totsuka Hikosuke. Even after the Meiji Restoration of 1868 the dojo still had famous members including Totsuka Hikosuke himself who was still fit and well. His successor was Totsuka Eibi who trained some very skilful students. He based himself in Chiba and from there reigned with his jujitsu.

About 1887-88 a big championship was hosted by the Keishicho and it was natural that the Totsuka people would fight the Kodokan people whose fame was growing. When the match was held in 1888 the Totsuka team consisted of 14 -15 members and the Kodokan put up the same number as I recall. Five of the Kodokan representatives fought others from different jujitsu schools and ten fought the Totsuka people. The Totsuka group included 'technicians' such as Terashima Taro and Nishimura Teijo (Sadasuke?). In this match Yamashita Yoshiaki of the Kodokan fought Terashima, Sato Hoken (Kodokan) fought Nishimura and Kawaai fought Katayama. Surprisingly these three matches ended in draws but the rest of the matches were won by the Kodokan. The Kodokan people were strong but I did not think that they would get such good results. I believe they won with [superior] spirit. The Totsuka people were strong and highly trained and not ones to be easily beaten. Before the Imperial Restoration of 1868 the Totsuka School reigned supreme but after the match above the Kodokan gradually unveiled its superiority.

The following also happened after the match I believe. At the time one of the Totsuka people was a jujitsu instructor at the Chiba Prefect prison. Following an invitation from Funakoshi Bei, the governor of the prefecture, I went along with a top student to explain the Kodokan educational method. What remains strongly in my memory is that after the explanations Saigo Shiro did randori with somebody and Totsuka Eibi, who was watching, said, "He is a master of jujitsu." I felt very satisfied when I heard him say that. The reputation of the Totsuka (Yoshin-ryu) school was very high indeed which both my former jujitsu teachers of the Tenjinshinyo and Kito schools had previously confirmed'[50].

In the *Kodokan Enkakuryaku* (Abbreviated History of the Development of the Kodokan) it states that the Yayoi Shrine in Shiba park in Tokyo, the shrine for Keishicho police and for those who followed their masters by committing suicide, organised *Budo Taikai* (martial arts competitions) in the Yayoi-kan to which all the strongest martial artists were invited. This was from the year 1885 and was to promote the fighting spirit of the police[51].

It would seem from the previous excerpts and the differing dates, names and venues, that the Totsuka jujitsu-ka most likely met the Kodokan judo-ka a number of times over the period 1884 –1888, either at the Keishicho HQ or elsewhere[52]. About the same time the Dai Nippon Butokukai was formed (1895), and began running its own martial arts competitions (Dai Enbu-kai), although it took until 1899 to come up with a set of competition rules.

It is not known what rules, if any, the match was held under. The fact that one Kodokan account claims to have won the match by small throws makes one wonder whether Kano had persuaded the Yoshin-ryu people to accept the rules which were later to be accepted by the Butokukai in 1899.

After the establishment of the Butokukai and Kodokan rules, jujitsu schools had the choice of fighting under the Butokukai rules or the Kodokan rules, which were very similar, but in fact a number of jujitsu schools outside Kyoto and Tokyo chose not to join either organisation but carried on promoting their traditional jujitsu under their own rules of engagement.

This match or matches has often been betrayed as the great confrontation between the Kodokan and jujitsu but in fact confronting

---

[50] Cf. Sakko. Vol 6. No.7.
[51] See Keishicho-shiko. Vol. 15.
[52] Cf. Oimatsu Judo Gojunen.

both of them was the national martial arts umbrella organization known as the Butokukai. One of the objectives of the Butokukai was to standardise (toitsu) kenjitsu and jujitsu both of which consisted of a myriad of styles. Kenjitsu for example was boiled down to one kata in 1912. Kano rightly perceived that this was the real battleground and infiltrated the Butokukai. It helped of course to have 'won' the match against the Totsuka Yoshin jujitsu.

One very differing account of the famous match is to be found in *Hiroku Nippon Judo* (Confidential Memoir on Japanese Judo) by Kudo which says that in the Totsuka Yoshin-ryu jujitsu versus Kodokan judo match, jujitsu won overwhelmingly on the ground. It is interesting that Kano's own account of the match has different dates and is fairly low key and matter of fact.

There is one story from Kano which perhaps points indirectly to the problems he was having with jujitsu. He wrote,

'In order to make my dojo stronger I thought I would like to have some physically stronger people in the dojo. In other words I did not only want skilful people. I heard that sumo people often recruited around Kujukuri in Chiba prefecture, so one day I took off with Saigo to that area but found nobody. Thereafter I constantly looked for stronger students but it wasn't easy to find them. Then I heard of a very strong fifteen year old. I met him with his parents and got their agreement to make him a student but he was a weak-willed child, not much good at judo, so I let him return home. Later on when stopping off on a train for Otsu I saw a big youth standing there. He trained with me for four years but eventually proved more suitable for commerce[53]'

Kudo also wrote in his Confidential Memoir on Japanese Judo about the match between Saigo Shiro of the Kodokan and Terashima of the Yoshin-ryu:

'Terashima was in his prime. He stood 172cm tall and weighed 82kg. [Saigo stood 5 feet tall and early pictures of him show him to be quite slight]. Saigo was the technician whereas Terashima was the

[53] See Kano Chosakushu Vol 3.

powerhouse. Saigo was renowned for his Yama-arashi and Ouchigari and Terashima was renowned for his Uchimata, Harai-goshi and Osotogari. Both were left-handed fighters. The match commenced and continued for fifteen minutes with strong attacks from both. The sweat began to pour off both men. Then Terashima approached Saigo somewhat carelessly and Saigo seizing his chance spun in for a big Yama-arashi which picked Terashima up and dumped him down on the mat'.

Note that there was no mention of groundwork.

In his novel *Sugata Sanshiro*, which was based on the exploits of Saigo Shiro, Tomita the author wrote that that his fictional hero Sugata Sanshiro threw Terashima so that, 'He was unable to stand up after the throw, had turned pale and at one point lost consciousness'. This outraged jujitsu-ka Kunii who later challenged Tomita on this. Tomita replied that he wrote a novel, not a history, and of course he exaggerated his hero's abilities. According to another author, Makino, who also wrote about Saigo, 'Yama-arashi was neither a Kodokan nor Yoshin-ryu technique but came from the Sekiguchi ryu where it was known as Yama-otoshi. Kano changed its name'. However it seems that Saigo did throw Terashima over with his Yama-arashi[54].

The Masago-cho era and first European trip (1889-91)

In 1889 Viscount Shinagawa returned from his ambassadorial post in Germany making Kano's use of his residence somewhat difficult, and this coincided with Kano resigning his teaching position at the Gakushuin due to differences with Viscount Lt General Miura the new head. However, forces were at work behind the scenes and he received an Imperial Household Agency order to spend a year or more on an educational research trip to Europe[55]. (See Chapter 13 – Kano's Trips Abroad). This meant he had to rapidly find another home for his dojo and school.

Friends and students quickly stepped in and through the mediation of Viscount Shinagawa and Vice-minister of the Army Katsura Taro, Kano

[54] See *Jujitsu Kyohan* by Anegawa.
[55] Note that this was an Imperial Household Agency order not a government order.

gained permission to rent a single-storey wooden building belonging to the army in Masago-cho in Hongo ward[56]. Here he was able to establish a 70-mat dojo to which he transferred his Kodokan. At the same time he rented a house in Kami-niban-cho in Kojimachi ward and there he transferred his own school (Kano-juku) and his 40-mat Shinagawa residence dojo which he called the Kodokan Kojimachi branch.

In September of 1889 Kano set sail on a foreign ship for Europe from Yokohama. Before departing he entrusted the management of his Kano-juku school and the Kodokan to three students while he was away in Europe. They were Iwanami Josho, Honda Masujiro and Saigo Shiro.

Sixteen months later in January 1891 Kano returned from his educational investigation of Europe (see Chapter 13 – Kano's trips abroad). On his return he discovered that discipline had been relaxed at the dojo and school and this led him to expel Saigo Shiro. He also had to hurriedly vacate his Masago-cho dojo since the army required it back, so he moved his school and dojo back to Kami-niban-cho (Kojimachi,) which then became the main dojo. This period became known as the 2nd Kami-niban-cho era. Kano briefly lodged with his older sister Yanagi Katsuko in her Yanagi-mansion in Azabu and entrusted the direct management of the Kodokan to a manager. With regard to his other Kano-juku students he kept in touch by lecturing them once a week in manners and how to conduct themselves. Note that Kano did not necessarily shut down a dojo when he moved to a new one. Often he used the old dojo for different educational purposes or just as a branch dojo.

To Kumamoto (1891-93)

A few months later in August 1891 Kano was appointed head of the Number 5 Upper Middle-school (Koto Chugakko) in Kumamoto on the southern island of Kyushu and also made Counsellor (*Sanjikan*) of the Ministry of Education.

Japan is composed of many islands. The biggest is Honshu which is regarded as the mainland and after that come Kyushu, Shikoku and Hokkaido. These are the main land masses of Japan. Kumamoto is one of the largest cities on the island of Kyushu and stands in a wide plain on the

---

[56] Katsura was a soldier-politician who later became Prime Minister and Commander of the Japanese Army.

Above: An early jujitsu restraint technique.

Above: A later jujitsu defence move.

Right: Sumo or judo?

Above: Surrounded by young judo students, Kano (second from right) and Yokoyama Sakujiro 8th Dan (second from left) see off 1st Lieutenant Hirose to Russia and 1st Lieutenant Takarabe to England, 1900.

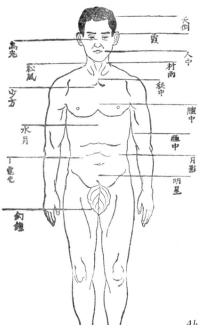

Above: Mifune (later 10th Dan) in his heyday.

Above: Chart showing the vital atemi nerve spots of the body.

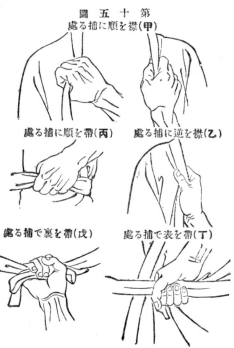

Right: Some interesting early judo grips.

Above left: Kano Jigoro demonstrating his favourite Ukigoshi on Yamashita, (Note the length of Kano's jacket.)

Above right: Note the old style judogi with short sleeves and trousers.

Left: Kano Jigoro in shizentai (natural posture) wearing the modern-looking judo suit which was redesigned in 1906.

Above: Kano conducting the Kodokan Promotion Ceremony.

Above: Mass mid-winter training in the
Shitatomizaka-cho dojo.

river Shira. The city was founded with the building of a castle at the end of the 16th century. It was regarded as one of the greatest feudal strongholds in all Japan. It then had a population of about 100,000. The people of Kyushu had long been regarded as tough individualists and the western feudal clans (Choshu and Satsuma) which were based there aided the return of the Emperor in 1868.

This was potentially a very difficult period for Kano. He had left his position at one of the most influential schools in the country with all its many connections and had had to move out of his dojo in Fujimi-cho. Help was at hand with an army building which he could rent to house his dojo, and then came an Imperial order to make a long investigational trip to Europe and this was in the days before good telecommunications and aviation. No sooner had he returned from Europe than he was shipped off to the provinces which he initially regarded as a retrograde career move. However, he was tempted by the possibility of being involved in setting up a Kyushu University. Fate was conspiring to keep him away from his Tokyo dojo. The Japanese Ministry of Education was no doubt wondering where to place this talented but stubborn teacher.

In September 1891 Kano took up office in his new school and instantly began promoting judo in Kumamoto. One of the first things he did was to set up a dojo in the storeroom of the headmaster's quarters and another one above the students' waiting room which he named *Zuina-kan*. His assistant was Kimotsuke Munetsugu who had accompanied him from Tokyo. Kimotsuke was reputed to be physically very strong. In a match against Kumamoto jujitsuka he tossed them down one after another which added to his and Kano's fame in Kyushu. It was said that Kimotsuke joined the Kodokan after a match against Munakata of the Kodokan in which Munakata handled him with ease.

Kano wrote about Kumamoto as follows: 'Kumamoto is a lively place for the Japanese martial arts (*bugei*). It was said that to succeed as head of the house a samurai had to have many certificates of proficiency in the various martial arts'. Kano knew that without a proper dojo in the school there would have been no evidence of training in his judo[57]. In the area there were a few dojos where jujitsu was taught by traditional teachers. Kano could not afford to set up a separate dojo so he did it on his school

[57] Presumably he wanted to issue his own judo/jujitsu certificates.

campus. Fortunately Kimotsuke accompanied him and helped with the judo instruction.

Teaching at the Kumamoto No. 5 School at the time was Lafcadio Hearn. He was an Irishman who had adopted the Japanese name of Koizumi Yakumo and often came to the dojo to watch. He was one of the first foreigners to write about Japan and about Kano's jujitsu and judo. He published a treatise on Kano's 'Jujitsu', which he included in his book Out of the East, published in Boston in 1895.

In January of 1893 Kano was re-appointed Ministry of Education counsellor and head of the Minister's Secretariat Library (in charge of school textbook authorisation), and returned to Tokyo to set up house in Ushigome, Sadohara-cho. In this house he boarded his Kano-juku younger group of students and the rest he transferred to Kami-niban-cho. The building in Kami-niban-cho was narrow and there was not enough space to lay all the 70 mats transported from the Masago-cho dojo so about 30 mats lay stacked up in one corner of the dojo.

The 1st Shita-tomizaka-cho era (1893-1906)

From time to time houses in Shita-tomizaka-cho came up for sale, and, very fortunately, in 1893 Kano was able to buy one and and build a new dojo of over 100 mats. This move to the 100-mat dojo was perhaps *the* turning point of the Kodokan's fortunes. A 100-mat dojo is a respectable size (14m x 14m), taking perhaps twenty or more free-fighting couples.

This period coincided with the Russo-Japanese war of 1904-5 in which Japan was successful. Yet again patriotic fervour spread throughout the country and the numbers wanting to learn judo jumped. At each stage of the Kodokan's growth it was not long before a bigger and better dojo was required. In November of that year the Kano-juku and the Kodokan moved into the newly completed dojo. This was the beginning of the Shita-tomizaka-cho (13 year) Era.

In 1894 the New Year's Day Ceremony was held on 1st January, and then on 6th of January the Kangeiko (Mid winter practice) began. On 14th January the Kagamibiraki Ceremony was held. On 20th May a splendid Dojo Inauguration Ceremony took place. Famous martial artists from all parts of the country were welcomed along with guests such as Katsu Awa, Shinagawa Yajiro (politician), Tanaka Koken, Takasaki Masakaze (poet and confidant of the Emperor), Itami Juken, Miyoshi Taizo and

Watanabe Nobiru. Kano himself talked about the history of Kodokan judo
and its future organisation and mission. Kata and randori was performed
by judo students, and masters of other jujitsu styles performed their kata
adding to the magnificence of the occasion.

Kano himself performed a Kodokan kata with Oda Katsutaro. The Zen
and fencing master Katsu Yasuyoshi (Kaishu) who witnessed this was
deeply moved by the display and on returning home wrote in beautiful
brush calligraphy the secret principles of Kodokan judo. This he expressed
in the words, *Mushin ni shite shizen no myo ni iri – mui ni shite henka no shin
o kiwamu*. ('In the state of no-mind enter the mystery of nature – without
intention, penetrate the God of change'). This was mounted and framed
and hung over the place of honour in the dojo, where it hangs to this
day.

Wanting to apply himself closely to the instruction of his students,
Kano moved into his new dojo and set up his quarters there. The annual
events of the Kodokan gradually got more and more splendid. In 1894
Kano created a Deliberation Council (*Shingi-kai*) to which he appointed
as members Yamashita Yoshiaki, Tomita Tsunejiro, Iwasaki Hoken, Kano
Tokusaburo, Kawai Keijiro, Iwanami Josho, Oda Katsutaro, Oshima
Hidesuke, Ura Taro, Shitate Tetsujiro and others.

Kodokan entry regulations

In 1896 the Kodokan entry regulations (*Kodokan Nyumon Kisoku*) were
revised as follows:

1. Those desirous of joining the Kodokan must present to the manager
   a completed application form and a CV
2. Those who are permitted to join must sign the Five Article Oath
   (see Chapter 5 – The Five Article Oath)
3. Those who gain permission to join must present one folding fan
   (*Ogi*) with a one yen joining fee. However no monthly tuition fee
   is charged.

What was noteworthy about this revision was Article 3 of the revised
Kodokan Entry Regulations. Kano believed that the Way (of judo) should
not mix with money, and that teaching should be given only to those
desirous of learning. This idea was based on the original spirit of the

Kodokan and an instruction fee was not levied. However, as the number of students increased and the dojo became more expensive to run, from 1904 onwards a dojo fee of 10 Sen was levied each month to cover a portion of the running costs. Note that this was some 22 years after the founding of the Kodokan. In the early days Kano supported the institution out of his own pocket. (See also Chapter 6 – Judo and Money). About this time Kano formed a Kodokan Club to promote friendship among his students. Meetings were held on the third Sunday of every odd-numbered month. The fee for this was three sen per month. (One sen = one hundredth of a yen).

Rules for Kodokan trainees

The Regulations for Trainees (*Shugyosha Kokoroe*) were also laid down in 1894:

1. Those who do judo must pledge to benefit the state and mankind through the training of their bodies
2. On entering and leaving the dojo a bow is to be made towards the place of honour (*joseki*)
3. When in the dojo the directions of the Master, teachers, officials and senior ranks are to be obeyed
4. Etiquette is to be maintained towards the teachers, senior grades and officials. Advanced judoka must look after and lead the less advanced, and they in turn must follow this lead
5. On entering the dojo, judoka must sign the register
6. Unreasonable absence is not permitted unless on account of illness or other unavoidable reasons. However those desirous of training must gain permission in advance
7. Change of guarantor or address is to be notified
8. Dress should be Japanese or western style dress
9. No nakedness is allowed outside the changing rooms. Smoking is not allowed
10. When in the dojo sit or stand correctly. Do not sit with knees sticking up, lie down, have hands in pockets or sit with legs stretched out
11. Those living in Tokyo should present to their teacher and colleagues one piece of *kagami-mochi* rice cake as a New Year gift

12. Those living afar or those ill should send New Year greetings by post and inform of new address

13. All judoka should participate in the spring and autumn Red and White contests (*Kohaku-shiai*) and in the monthly contests (*Tsukinami-shiai*)

14. Conform to the true spirit of judo, always foster a sincere heart, respect morality, discharge your duties, be prudent in your conduct, be hygienic, and, with regard to all things, be of right mind.

The first and last articles were and still are regarded as the most important.

Mid-summer training (*Shochugeiko*)

In July 1896 the first of the Mid-summer training periods (Shochugeiko) were held and have continued till this day. The length of this testing training during the hottest and most humid time of the year is 30 days. The high humidity makes it difficult to breathe and for most of the 30-day period trainees rarely manage to dry out their judogi. Drinking of water during the training is not allowed.

The Great Randori

One of the most talked-about events of this period was the demonstration randori between Yokoyama 6th Dan and Nagaoka 4th Dan at the Kagamibiraki ceremony of 1899. Both were later promoted to 10th Dan.

Yokoyama Sakujiro started off as a student of Tenjinshinyo jujitsu under the hammer of Inoue Keitaro. In 1886, at the age of sixteen, he became a student at the Kodokan where he rapidly rose through the ranks to reach 6th Dan aged 28 in 1898. At that point it was said that he had never been beaten.

Nagaoka Hidekaze joined the Kodokan in 1893 and reached the rank of 4th Dan aged 23 in 1898. The magazine Kokushi recorded the randori which was the last item of the ceremony as follows:

'The two men calmly entered the full venue to thunderous applause. On the one hand was the older battle-hardened Yokoyama who had never been beaten, and on the other hand the young and up-and-coming skilful Nagaoka.

The most noteworthy thing after they came to grips was how

skilfully Yokoyama countered the ankle sweep of Nagaoka with his own foot sweep (*ashi-barai-gaeshi*). Nagaoka looked as if he would fall but nimbly twisted his body and sat facing his opponent. This lightning like reaction was so fast that spectators were barely able to recognise it.

The randori proceeded with Nagaoka coming in with his favourite *Yoko-sutemi-waza* (side sacrifice throw) which dropped Yokoyama neatly on his side causing the spectators to gasp. The technique was regarded as valid.

This was a demonstration randori, and not a question of who would win or lose, but such was the level of Nagaoka's skill that Kano graded him to 5th Dan on the day.'

Apart from the instant promotion of Nagaoka, twelve other men were graded to 4th Dan that day including Yuasa Takejiro.

That the randori was 'decided' with a foot sweep counter and a side body sacrifice throw gives us a glimpse of what the randori was like at the time. The side body sacrifice throws seemed to have featured highly in early judo and in jujitsu. In the UK under Koizumi for example, *yoko-sutemi* throws were limited to senior grades for some time because they caused a fair number of elbow, shoulder and leg injuries (either to the opponent or other trainees standing nearby).

The use of the *Ashibarai*-counter (aka *Tsubame-gaeshi*) indicates perhaps the prevalence of *ko-waza* (small techniques) at that time. It was not till after 1906 when the judogi was redesigned that the *O-waza* (big techniques) began to emerge (see Chapter 12 – Big Throws and the Re-designed Judogi).).

More career moves

In 1893 Kano was appointed head of the No 1 Upper Middle School in Tokyo (*Koto-chu-gakko*), Ministry of Education counsellor (in charge of the Special Educational Affairs Bureau) and then in September of the same year, head of the Teacher Training College in Tokyo (*Tokyo Koto Shihan Gakko*).[58] This Teacher Training College (for male teachers of secondary education) was at that time the only one in the whole country, making it a very influential post. Kano became head when very little work had been

---

[58] Known in the USA and France as a Higher Normal School.

done on its fundamental strategies and objectives. Kano applied himself and shaped them. At first Kano was not too keen on the job, but soon realised how important it was and went at it with a will.

To start with this college only consisted of 15 teachers and some 80 students divided into three classes and a small budget, but the job was much bigger than it looked. Along with the college came an attached middle school, primary school, music school and educational museum. In effect Kano had the chance to lead a whole new generation of Japanese secondary school teachers which he seized with alacrity. For a short while Kano was loaded with three jobs at the same time, not to mention running the Kodokan as well.

Kano stayed in position as head of the Tokyo Teacher Training College (Koto-shihan-gakko) for a 27 year span between 1893 and 1920 with three short breaks, totalling three years, in between. During one of the short breaks he was appointed head of the Ministry of Education's General Educational Affairs Bureau for about one year. In 1901 he was re-appointed head of the Tokyo Teacher Training College for the third time in which position he stayed for 19 years up to 1920. (Kano is said by some non-Japanese writers to have briefly been Minister of Education but I can find no Japanese source for this).

Kano said in one of his lectures that he noticed that physically fit teachers who participated in sports were much admired (and listened to) by the students, so he made sure that all his trainee teachers participated in sporting and physical activities. He went on to create a strong physical education course at the college which hosted many sporting events. See also Chapter 13 – Kano, physical education and the Olympics.

Critical mass

Perhaps the key advances during this period were first the enlargement of the dojo to 100 mats in 1893 – a new physical and moral combat method is offset by a grand dojo. Secondly the jujitsu challenge diminished. Thirdly war against the Russians proved successful and this resurrected Japanese confidence so that many young Japanese sought to train at the new modernised jujitsu known as Kodokan judo under its inspiring founder. And finally Kano found the job that was to occupy him for over thirty years in the Tokyo Teacher Training College. The numbers grew and the Kodokan was virtually unstoppable.

Chapter 8
Judo in Education and Women's Judo

In Chapter 2 we saw how the ex-samurai class disliked the new foreign style of physical training (*taiso*) and pushed for the introduction of jujitsu and kenjitsu into schools. The argument was strong. What need do we have, they said, for foreign physical jerks when we have such fine traditional training methods already. The Ministry of Education initiated an investigation into both but the investigation came down against the introduction of either into the school curriculum saying that they had more disadvantages than advantages. However the Ministry did allow jujitsu to continue in a few middle schools which had already begun using it. This was in 1883 which was barely one year after the Kodokan had been founded. The jujitsu of that time was probably quite rough and ready and in fact not that suitable for school children but Kano perhaps saw an opportunity here and began working for the introduction of a suitably modified jujitsu into schools now that the prospect had been raised.

School and University Judo

It took quite a long time to place judo/jujitsu and kenjitsu/gekken/kendo into the school curriculum. In 1911 jujitsu/judo was placed in the middle school curriculum and in 1931 it became part of teacher training education. In fact it was not till 1926 that the name of judo officially replaced the term jujitsu. However, in the meantime judo was practised by many young male adults in the Kodokan, university clubs or in the street dojos (machi dojos). There are scattered references to juniors practising judo but not in a big way. School would have been the place to do it but first it had to be formally accepted by the Japanese Ministry of Education.

At that time in Japan and for many decades afterwards, 'sport' as leisure was a concept that barely existed. Life was too serious and a good reason for doing something like judo had to be provided or it might be regarded as frivolous. Even today most sport in Japan is done at school or university.

Once education is over it is down to the hard business of work, marriage and providing for the family.

No doubt the fact that Kano introduced extra-curricular judo into such prestigious institutions as the Peers College and the Imperial Tokyo University helped judo enormously. He literally started at the top. At the inauguration ceremony of the Peers College in 1883 which the Emperor Meiji attended, Kano demonstrated his judo. It is almost certain that Imperial court officials would have vetted the inclusion of the judo display beforehand because the Emperor's presence could be seen as an endorsement of judo as happened, for example, when he attended sumo events.

Kano's promotion of judo in schools and colleges proceeded at a rapid pace. By 1887 judo was practised in over 12 major institutions in Tokyo and in over 16 educational establishments outside. Wherever Kano went in his work judo sprang up, and gradually judo appeared in other parts of the country as well.

Where Kano or his students had no direct input, the practise of judo and kendo began, like baseball and rowing, with interested students spontaneously creating extra-curricular training groups. These then formed into recognised departments within the college with alumni associations forming thereafter. Competitions in and between schools developed quickly. These usually included demonstrations of kata and exhibition matches by top judoka.

From quite early on attempts were made to pass legislation making judo/jujitsu and kenjitsu/*gekken* compulsory in schools[59]. It was a time of nationalist fervour and obviously a good case could be made for their inclusion since they consisted of fighting techniques which would have been useful in battle as well as creating fit and strong students. Kano was well placed in the world of education and was able to influence the legislation, both personally and through his high-placed connections, to keep judo on the right track. Despite the worsening international situation

Kano seems to have managed to keep his judo as a learning vehicle or form of education. The militarists no doubt wanted to make it more directly applicable to the battlefield.

Eventually judo or kendo became *compulsory* for all primary and secondary students which created a massive participation base that other 'sports' did not enjoy. It was not till after the Pacific War that this monopoly was removed, making way for a wider variety of other sports and martial arts in schools. Some might say that this was when Japanese judo was most seriously weakened.

Although junior judo existed from the start of the Kodokan it does not seem to have existed in large numbers. From the beginning the Kodokan had a few juniors whose starting age was eight or nine. Paralleling the introduction of judo into the schools curriculum a special junior section was set up in the Kodokan in 1934. This consisted of 50 juniors aged ten to 16. In the same year the Kodokan junior section hosted the first Tokyo Metropolitan Junior Judo championships in which 37 schools participated. Further competitions were held but soon the worsening international situation caused them to stop.

As we have seen judo had an early start in higher education at the top Tokyo Imperial University where Kano not only studied but taught judo. As the university system expanded, more and more university dojos started up[60]. Like some American universities where ability in football or baseball guarantees smooth entry a number of Japanese universities were the breeding grounds of future national and international judo champions. These college judomen were in the prime of their lives and the training was hard, non-stop and spirited for four years. Not all universities were strong at judo, some concentrated on different sports and traditional arts entirely, but once a university dojo acquired a reputation, competition to enter it grew considerably. When the four years of university were finished the students moved on into the wider world of work, although some gifted ones carried on as judo teachers.

Judo teacher training

In Japan and in many parts of the world it was and still is common for judoka to become teachers by first acquiring a black belt then teaching

---

[60] In the 1960s there were over fifty universities in Tokyo.

without any other qualifications – in other words they learned to teach by doing it. Most Japanese would probably have got their 1st Dan black belt at middle school or around the age of 16 but would be unlikely to teach. Teaching would be left to the older more experienced judoka.

However basic technique was standardised, particularly in the Kata, Gokyo and later in the Kodokan Designated Technique list[61]. The Tai-otoshi taught in Tokyo would be same as the one taught in Hokkaido. This, along with basic principles such as Seiryoku Zenyo, Ju, Kuzushi and Shizentai plus plenty of randori, would represent basic judo instruction. Beyond that the older and higher graded teachers (*sensei*) would hand out tips on technique to the students. Modern theories of how to teach and exercise physiology would have been a small part of the early judo teachers' training package although once judo became a compulsory subject on the school curriculum proper qualifications would have become necessary. By and large judo experience was valued more than theoretical knowledge.

Early attempts to standardize the teaching of judo began about 1911 when the Kodokan set up the Kodokan Judo Teacher Training School (*Kodokan Judo Kyoin Yoseisho*), providing a three year course for suitably educated students of middle school education and above who wanted to become judo teachers. Apart from judo technique the students also studied ethics and biology. This course was later phased out.

Somewhat late in the day an Advanced Judo Teacher Training School (*Koto Judo Kyoin Yoseisho*) was established at the Kodokan in 1939. The one year course accommodated 40 students of 4th dan grade and above. This continued till 1945 when it was abolished because of the Second World War.

In addition to this, other educational institutions created specialist schools or faculties for judo teacher training. Among the educational ones were the Tokyo Teacher Training College headed by Kano, Tokyo Special Physical Education College and in the non-educational sector were the Butokukai Specialist Martial Arts College – Busen for short, and the Kokushikan Specialist College (*Kokushikan Senmon Gakko*).

The first physical education college in Japan was the Ministry of Education's Physical Exercise School (*Taiso Denshujo*), set up in 1879. This

[61] Kodokan Shitei-waza.

school became attached to the predecessor of the Tokyo Teacher Training College (*Tokyo Koto Shihan Gakko*) in 1885, and then became part of the Training College itself when Kano was appointed head[62]. To start with the PE course was for only one year but like physical education in most countries it changed to a three or four year course, consisting of the physical part (centering on judo or kendo in Japan's case) with other compulsory arts and science subjects. Later some of the above institutions merged to become the present-day Tokyo Education University (Tokyo Kyoiku Daigaku) from which famous judoka such as Inokuma Isao and Sato Nobuyuki emerged.

In 1905 the Butokukai created a martial arts teacher training school based on Judo and Kendo and other general subjects. In 1911 this was replaced by a martial arts school for advanced teacher training in Budo, the national language, and classical Chinese. In the following year this school was renamed the Specialist Martial Arts School (*Bujitsu Senmon Gakko*) and received its specialist school licence. From this time until 1947, when it was banned by the Allied Occupation Forces, the school produced many fine teachers[63].

Women's judo

There are scattered early references to women doing judo in Japan. Perhaps the earliest was to one Yasuda in 1904. Women's judo classes first began in 1923 under the instruction of Honda 6th Dan, although Kano is said to have privately taught four or five women about this time. Prior to this he had obviously thought about training methods for women, as can be seen in the reasons he gave for creating the Ju-no-kata. As a result of this experience with teaching women Kano opened a two week summer school in his personal dojo in 1925, where he taught 12 women from different parts of the country. In 1931 a Women's Section was created at Kodokan. New female members were required to swear the Kodokan Oath and affix their seal to the Register, the same as the men. Among those registering at the time were Kosaki Kawako (the first woman 1st Dan – in 1933) and Noritomi Masako, who subsequently became 5th

---

[62] This small section of physical education history explains Kano's later important role in Japanese physical education.

[63] Cf Judo Gojunen by Oimatsu.

Dan in 1940. Thereafter the number of Japanese women judoka slowly grew. In 1945 there were 22 female black belts in grades 1st to 5th Dan but after the Pacific War the numbers increased substantially. In 1955 there were 642 registered Kodokan female members including 82 Dan grades.

Certainly women's presence in Japanese judo was very small for many years. Judo would seem to have been an almost exclusive male preserve. Outside Japan, women's participation steadily increased in most parts of the world especially with the rapid development of women's judo competitions. Europe and America were ahead of Japan in this respect. Women competed in the Olympic Games from 1992, in the world championships from 1980 and in the European championships from 1975.

Chapter 9
The Dai-Nippon Butokukai

At this point, however, it becomes necessary to devote some space to the *Dai-Nippon Butokukai* (Butokukai for short) which from 1895 to 1947 played an important role in judo's history.

Apart from its historical role in Japanese judo, some words on the Butokukai will help clear up a major puzzle. There was a suspicion among some non-japanese judoka training in Japan that tensions existed historically within Japanese judo especially after the Pacific war. What they were was never made clear. For example in the UK in the 1950s, a London club engaged an extremely competent Japanese judoka by the name of Abe Kenshiro 6th Dan. It soon became obvious that his view of judo and its principles was somewhat different to the Kodokan view. The judo looked basically the same but the principles were different[64]. This puzzled a number of British judoka, who having been taught by Kodokan men or having read books mostly produced by Kodokan people thought they knew all about judo. As it turns out Abe was the product of the Kyoto Butokukai Busen (Kyoto Butokukai Specialist Martial Arts College) and winner of a number of major contests. It was said that he even beat the great Kimura once.

At its simplest the Butokukai was a semi-governmental body created to control the Japanese martial arts. This brought it into conflict with the Kodokan which represented only one martial art. As we know Kodokan judo survived and the Butokukai did not. Beyond that the basic conflict here was possibly between Budo (the martial Way) and Judo (the compliant Way). Kano's concept of ju-do was more akin to the classical Chinese jou-tao or the way of compliance and deference and the Tokugawa concept of Bunbu Ryodo (the dual paths of war *and* peace). No

---

[64] Abe had a reputation for being an individualist both in Japan and the UK so his theories (kyushin-do and banbutsu ruten) on judo may well have been his own.

doubt the Budoka thought that times were dangerous as indeed they were and that more stress should be placed on Bu rather than Bun.

While Kano was alive he was able to promote his judo with its strong compliant and educational slant through his position, personal prestige and his influential friends but increasingly the war situation and then his demise meant that more emphasis was placed on judo as a combat form and promoter of the Budo spirit. From the year of Kano's death in 1938 to 1947 when the Butokukai was abolished a vacuum was created which the Butokukai filled although the war overshadowed everything.

The origin of the Butokukai

We have seen the early Tokyo Metropolitan Police's use of jujitsu for police training (See Chapter 2 – From jujitsu to judo – the Early Shoots) and its sponsorship of annual martial arts competitions. However, at the turn of the century, the Japanese government lacked control of its many martial arts and their students, which in the past would have been regulated by the *Hangaku* (clan schools) system with the secret police (*Metsuke*). The establishment of the Butokukai coincided with the Sino-Japanese war of 1894-95, when a patriotic mood swept the country. In fact the announcement of the setting up of the new organization was made on the day that a peace treaty between Japan and China was signed. Promotion of the martial arts was regarded as useful for the war effort against China (and later Russia) and for fostering fighting spirit.

The Kodokan organisation had grown considerably, but as a private organisation dedicated to one martial art it had limitations, and the government evidently felt the need to promote and standardise all of the military skills throughout the whole country. Consequently, in 1895 the Dai-Nippon Butokukai was formed with its headquarters in Kyoto. The first president was a member of the Imperial family and its officials were drawn from the upper ranks of the military, from senior provincial officials and from prominent martial artists. Kano, it seems, was one of the originators and promoters of the idea from the early stages.

The stated purpose of the Butokukai was to promote the Martial Way (*Budo*) and the military virtues or morality (*Butoku*), and raise the military spirit (*Shiki*) of the Japanese. In addition to the general aims of the organisation the Butokukai pledged to build and maintain the Military Virtues Palace (*Butokuden*) in the grounds of the Heian Shrine in Kyoto, organise annual martial arts festivals (*Butoku-Matsuri*) and martial arts competitions (*Dai-Enbu-Kai*), install a school, dojo and other necessary Budo educational organs, award grades, honour those who excelled in the Martial Virtues and Way, build an arsenal and gather weapons, preserve old martial arts, edit and compile documents relating to the martial virtues, the martial way and its weapons and publish a magazine of the Society. It was in fact a national martial arts umbrella organisation which eventually established Butokuden branches throughout Japan as well as a specialist martial arts school in Kyoto (*Butokukai senmon gakko* or *Busen* for short).

The establishment of the Butokukai created a problem for the Kodokan, which in 1895 was only 13 years old with an estimated annual membership intake of about 400. Kano was working hard to promote his judo but the jujitsu people were resisting. Furthermore the Kodokan's objectives were somewhat different from that of the Butokukai. Kano stressed judo as a form of moral and physical *education* and as a combat art, but with the more dangerous techniques eliminated from its free-fighting form. The Butokukai on the other hand was more orientated towards *combat* and no doubt wanted the dangerous bits kept in. It also promoted the Budo philosophy which Kano did not talk much about, although he did stress *shiki* or martial spirit.

Kano set about making sure that he slotted into the Butokukai organisation right from the start and that his Kodokan judo dan grade system existed side by side with the Butokukai jujitsu grades. In 1898 Kano was invited to chair the Butokukai Jujitsu Competition Rules committee. In 1899 the new rules were produced and accepted (see below). Not long after Kano became a counsellor of the Butokukai in 1900.

Within the Butokukai a judo section was created to which Isogai (later 10th Dan) of the Kodokan was appointed as chief instructor in 1902 on Kano's recommendation. Isogai became a leading instructor of the Busen and Butokukai where he taught Kodokan judo. Nowadays we think of jujitsu and judo as separate entitities but about the time the Butokukai was founded, and for quite some time after, Kodokan judo would probably have been seen by the authorities as yet another jujitsu school, albeit a very successful one.

The Butokuden which the Butokukai pledged to rebuild and maintain was originally an ancient shrine devoted to the Bushin or the gods of war within the grounds of the Heian castle in Kyoto, where sumo, horse riding and archery were often demonstrated in front of the early emperors. It was burnt down in AD 975 but was then rebuilt in 986. Not much is known about it thereafter, but in 1895 – a thousand years later – it was resurrected on the same site as the home of the new Butokukai. It was a huge imposing temple-like building made of wood.

The first Butokukai festival and martial arts competition was held in 1895 and continued every year until 1944, when it was stopped by the war. Eventually in 1947 the Butokukai was abolished by the Allied forces under the Potsdam Agreement for being a hotbed of militarism and ultra-nationalism. (See Chapter 17 &The Dissolution of the Butokukai). At this point the Kodokan regained its total monopoly of judo in Japan that it lost in 1895.

Budo and Bushido

As seen above the objective of the Butokukai was to promote Budo (the military Way) and foster Shiki or the martial spirit. Kano himself stated that his judo promoted Shiki but appears to have avoided the use of the word Budo. So what was Budo – or the later word *Bushido* – which became controversial before, during and after the Pacific War?[65]

My large *Kojien* Japanese dictionary defines the older word *Budo* as:

1. The Way that the Bushi (warrior) should follow (*bushi no mamoru beki michi*)
2. Bushido [in other words Budo and Bushido are the same]
3. The Way of the Bow and Arrow (*Kyu-ya no michi*)
4. It's opposite:The Way of Peace (*Bun-do*) or more literally the Way of Writing or Civilisation.

Bushido, the more recent word, has a fuller definition:

1. The moral laws developed by the military class in Japan from the Kamakura period (1185-1333) and through the Tokugawa period (1603-1868) where it formed a Confucian ideological support of the feudal society. It stressed: loyalty, sacrifice, fidelity, integrity, etiquette, purity, simplicity, frugality, martial spirit, honour and devotion.

[65] The Second World War in south-east Asia was often called the Taiheiyo-senso or Pacific (Ocean) War by the Japanese.

The setting for Bushido was a feudal society in times of war, where warriors held land from a superior in exchange for military service and loyalty. It was a type of contract between two parties but with loyalty to the lord coming first.

Apart from the succession of Rules for the Warriors (Buke Sho Hatto) issued by the early Tokugawa military rulers, books such as *Budo Shoshinshu* (*Budo for Beginners*) by Daidoji Yuzan and works by Yamaga Soko (1622- 85) spelled out in more detail the essence of Budo/Bushido. The famous first sentence of the Budo Shoshin-shu runs, 'One who is a samurai must before all things keep constantly in mind, by day and by night ... that he has to die. That is his chief business.' If anything, the concept of being willing to die for one's honour, feudal lord, the Emperor or Japan became its chief feature. Calling upon the Budo spirit was a rallying cry which imposed a heavy load on those it was directed at.

Dying meant not only dying in battle but, where appropriate, suicide in a particularly painful manner: namely slitting one's own stomach and then having a friend or assistant behead you with his sword (*seppuku*). There are many instances of soldiers of different nationalities being ready to die in battle or commit suicide, such as the ancient Romans who fell upon their swords or the soldiers of the First World War who marched slowly into withering machine gun fire to die in their thousands but the Japanese took it to extreme lengths with seppuku.

The early emergence of the concept of Budo during the Kamakura period (1185-1333) had an immediate relevance as it was a time of war, however, when the concept began to strengthen in the Tokugawa period it coincided with a long era of peace that lasted from 1603 to 1868, so there was no immediate relevance for the philosophy. The *bushi* were instructed to train, act, look and think like warriors – but there were no wars to fight. If Japan had not isolated itself for over two centuries and had done what many Western nations were doing at that time, namely colonising the world, it might have had more application. Presumably any warlike spirit the samurai created had to be expended among themselves, with the other social classes taking care to stay out of their way.

Although there are crucial differences between the European concept of chivalry and Budo such as the chivalrous protection of women and the weaker members of society, the idea of the loyal, brave and virtuous warrior ready to die for his lord lodged in the Japanese psyche in the same way as the idea of King Arthur and the Knights of the Round Table did in England. The *sentiment* of Budo/bushido is perhaps what drives Budo more, even in modern Japan, than any clearly thought-out philosophy[66]. The word bushido became somewhat tainted in the 20th century following the perceived militaristic excesses of the Japanese armies in China and south-east Asia.

The Japanese were ready to die fighting and did so in large numbers, and the discipline they handed out was just as harsh on their own men as on those of other nationalities. One Japanese soldier's account of his war describes his almost daily beatings by superior officers to the extent that he felt that something was missing if he was not beaten[67].

The Butokukai jujitsu competition and judges' rules

Kano managed to get through the first 18 years of his organisation without any written contest or randori rules – at least none have been found. According to Kano, competitions were held during that time but the rules were fixed according to the particular circumstances. The Kodokan, however, had been doing lots of randori in its training right from the beginning and the necessary (unwritten?) rules for these made a ready prototype for later rules.

The Butokukai however jumped the gun by deciding to compile jujitsu rules for its annual competitions, known as the Dai-Enbu-kai, in 1899. However the decision to impose competition rules on the jujitsu schools began to move them in the same direction as judo. Judo was jujitsu with fighting rules. Jujitsu in the raw was without rules.

It has often been pointed out both by Japanese jujitsu and judo people that the big difference between jujitsu and judo was judo's randori and competition rules[68]. As Kano wrote there were crude forms of free-fighting in jujitsu but Kano's genius lay in devising a rule formula that allowed more or less injury-free free-fighting and it is clear that what judo people mostly liked about judo is the satisfaction and training they got from intensive free-fighting. Kodokan judo randori quickly established

---

[66] See *Japan: A short cultural history* by G.B.Sansom, pages 498 -517, for fuller discussion.
[67] From Shinkutai (*The Vacuum Zone*). The Japanese were mostly contemptuous of those who did not die fighting.
[68] See *Jujitsu Nyumon* by Kanno Hisashi

itself as a satisfying form of competitive exercise (sport) and at the same time the practise of kata declined drastically. The randori aim was to throw the opponent cleanly onto his back, restrain him on his back or gain a submission from a strangle or joint lock. This training method created very strong and durable physiques, was effective for self-defence and built character.

As both Kano and Isogai said, the jujitsu of their time tended to consist mostly of atemi and groundwork, and kata was the main way they trained, but as specialist jujitsu dojos developed in the early Meiji period (from 1868), the jujitsu-ka began to do less kata and more free-fighting, which tended to be mainly groundwork.

Both styles produced fit, strong grapplers. Kano thought it was important to stay on one's feet in combat but many jujitusu schools disagreed. The first great non-Japanese world champion, Anton Geesink of the Netherlands, once said, 'Randori is the soul of judo'. More than anything it was the free-fighting rules formulated by Kano that spread judo around the world. Bearing in mind the complete absence of any other coherent set of competitive rules these were a work of genius. He got it right, right from the start.

In 1899 the Butokukai appointed a committee chaired by Kano to formulate jujitsu competition rules from a draft which he had to first prepare. Also on this committee were Yamashita, Isogai and Yokoyama of the Kodokan, Handa Shotaro of the Daito-ryu, Hoshino Kumon of the Shiten-ryu, Totsuka Eibi of the Yoshin-ryu, Uehara of the Ryoishinto-ryu, Kondo Shutaro of the Kito-ryu, Samura Seimei of the Takeuchi Santo-ryu and Suzuki Sonhachiro of both the Sekiguchi and Yoshin ryu.

The rules that this committee had to formulate were for jujitsu competitions between the various existing jujitsu schools which stressed different aspects of unarmed combat. Probably the Butokukai did not want to deal with the many competing styles and was seeking to standardize them. The committee meetings were no doubt argumentative affairs with disputes about what should and should not be allowed (punching, kicking, leg-locks etc), on what surface and wearing what clothes. Exactly how the arguments went in committee is not known. This formulation of these rules was some 17 years after the establishment of the Kodokan. As will be seen in the next section the formal Kodokan Judo free-fighting and competition rules which surfaced within a year were virtually identical to the Butokukai jujitsu rules which leads one to believe that it was the Kano view of things that prevailed. The result was a set of rules that have withstood the test of time. The judo rules that we have now are not that different to the ones the Butokukai Rules Committee first formulated in 1899.

Old style jujitsu made great play on the fact that there were no rules in combat – anything was permissible. As testimony to this, note that up to the early Tokugawa period (early 17th century) the word *Shiai* (match or competition) which is nowadays written with the two characters *test* and *meet* was often written with the characters die (*shi*) and meet (*ai*). In other words it was sometimes a fight to the death. In fact judo's position was not that different. There were rules for training and competition but if it came to a *shinken shobu* (a real fight), anything went (see below).

In the early days of the Kodokan, contests were held to *test* the abilities of the students. Kano refereed the contests and certainly gave instruction in competition and randori. The match between the Kodokan and Totsuka Yoshin-ryu in 1885(?) at the Tokyo Metropolitan Police headquarters must have been fought under some rules agreed in advance, but unfortunately there is no surviving evidence of what the arrangements were. It would have been useful to know even if it was fought under no rules! In a fight or challenge of any kind it is necessary to know what is allowed or disallowed.

In 1900 Kano wrote, 'The regulation of combat was not originally decided by fixed rules. It was decided by the circumstances of the time and the abilities of the combatants. If it was a real fight (*shinken shobu*) it might be decided by the death of one party. In one respect judo randori is a real fight but since it is not a fight to the death it has to be done safely[69].'

Kano himself mentions in 1900 the earlier existence of Kodokan randori competition rules but there is no written record of them. Up to this point he would probably have judged the majority of contests himself. So the Butokukai may have jumped the gun, or it is quite possible that Kano worked behind the scenes to push for written rules through this semi-governmental body. Obviously Kano had some clear ideas about judo rules.

One set of jujitsu randori-competition rules survive from the 1887-97

[69] Kokushi. No.20.1900

period. These were used by Shinki-ryu Rentai Jujitsu School[70]. The first to get 15 points was the winner. Ten points were awarded for a good sacrifice (*sutemi*) throw and nine points for an incomplete one. Eight points were awarded for a good body throw such as o-goshi, seoi, uchimata etc and seven points for an incomplete one. Six points were awarded for a leg technique and five points for an incomplete one. Four points were awarded for a good technique outside the above categories and two points for an incomplete one. Finally two points were given for kumi-uchi techniques (such as *kesagata, bozu, kannuki*), strangles or for restraints (hold-downs) of over one minute, and one point was given for repeats.

The interesting points about this set of rules are firstly the emphasis given to the hierarchy of different throws, some of which were evidently regarded as heavier than others, and secondly the inclusion of the 'incomplete' technique which must be close to the waza-ari concept of judo.

The Butokukai jujitsu rules which the committee quickly prepared under Kano's chairmanship consisted of 13 articles:

1. In the Butokukai a jujitsu competition is decided on the basis of Nage-waza (throws) and Katame-waza (groundwork)
2. Nage-waza includes both standing techniques (tachiwaza) and sacrifice techniques (sutemi-waza) and Katame-waza (groundwork) includes both strangles (shime-waza), restraints (osae-waza) and joint-locks (kansetsu-waza)
3. The match is decided by [the first to get] two ippon scores.[71] If however both contestants have an ippon each the match will be decided by the third ippon
4. If after a suitable time the judges cannot decide who the winner is the contest will be stopped and the judge will call out Hikiwake (draw). The same will apply if both contestants have one Ippon apiece
5. When one contestant gains an ippon the judge will call out ippon. When a second Ippon is awarded (to him) the judge will call out nihon (two ippons) and finish the contest

[70] Cf. Judo Shiai Shimpan Kitei by Morishita & Murayama.
[71] Ippon means one-Hon. Hon is used in Judo for *counting* a full or complete technique.

6. When it is difficult to evaluate a throw as a full ippon, but when it has considerable value, or in groundwork when it is almost an ippon but the opponent just manages to escape, the judge can call waza-ari for the attacking party[72]. If after that there are one or more similar instances the judge can call at his discretion Awashite Ippon (two or more waza-ari combine to make an ippon) and award the score to the person concerned[73]. When there are a number of near misses (semi-scoring moves) by both contestants the judge can add them up and award a victory based on superiority. Once an ippon has been called the judge will not take into account any number of previous insufficient scores

7. A throw Ippon must fulfil the following criteria:
(a) A throw is scored when one side applies a technique and the opponent falls directly as a result of it or falls trying to escape from it, but no score is given if one side deliberately falls to the ground or falls in error
(b) The opponent must land face up (aomuke) regardless of type of technique or whether the technique can be correctly identified
(c) The throw must have considerable impetus and force

8. No score is given to the thrower or the thrown if either turns or twists in the air and avoids landing face up

9. No matter how quickly the opponent twists and returns to a convenient position after a clean throw it will be regarded as a loss for him[74]

10. If the opponent clings to or dangles from the thrower but is made to fall spectacularly the judge can decide it is a loss for him regardless of Article 7 of these rules

11. In groundwork if one party taps the mat or the opponent twice with a hand or foot and/or says *Mairi* (I am beaten) this will be regarded as a signal of defeat. However in Osae-waza the judge need not wait for the taps or *Mairi* and can decide when the opponent has been unable to rise to his feet after a suitable amount

---

[72] It is not clear whether the 'escape' is from a strangle, joint lock or restraint.

[73] Awashite Ippon means the same as the modern Awasete Ippon.

[74] An example of this would be the man who rolls quickly back onto his feet from a Sutemi-waza and tries to carry on competing.

    of time that an ippon has been won. With strangles (*shime-waza*) and joint-locks (*kansetsu-waza*) the judge can also decide before any signal of defeat is made that an ippon has been gained

12. Since the main purpose of Butokukai competion is to test the technical power of the contestants in throwing and groundwork, the judge should caution anyone who avoids coming to grips because he does not like groundwork. Similarly those who dislike throwing and who start kneeling or lying down without coming to grips in the standing position should also be directed to observe this rule

13. Toe, finger and ankle locks are not included among the (permissible) joint locks[75].

Between about1900 and 1925 most contests were called three-ippon contests (*sambon shobu*). The words Sambon shobu would be announced by the judge at the beginning of the match. However this referred to a best-of-three situation where a third ippon was fought for if both contestants had an Ippon each. There were some deviations from the rules. Juniors, for example, sometimes fought for three minutes and for only one ippon. Gradually the contests came to be called two-ippon contests (*Nihon Shobu*) to bring it more into line with reality. When both contestants had an Ippon each, the judge would call out *Ippon-shobu* and hopefully the match would then be decided by the next ippon. From about 1900, when time was short in a competition because of the number of contestants, competitions began to be fought for one ippon. Most of the Red and White contests in the Kodokan for example were fought for one ippon.

    Note that waza-ari was called for a near ippon but a second waza-ari call did not instantly add up to a full ippon as happens nowadays. It was up to the judge who could award the waza-ari for two or more near-misses or not at all. The use of the word 'more' became a bit of a problem. If a first near miss was a good 70% of an ippon that could be called waza-ari. But subsequent scores of say 40% and 30% of an ippon might be regarded by the referee as sufficient to call another waza-ari combining to make ippon.

---

[75] Presumably wrist, knee, neck and spine locks were allowed?

Kano said about the Ippon:

'In throwing or groundwork when there has been a technique that can be regarded as an Ippon that should then be called as such, but from time to time when one contestant makes a technique that is not a full ippon and goes on to do groundwork that almost scores, the combination of the two techniques could be regarded as an Ippon. The judge should make a calculation of the degree to which a score was made in each case and adding them together declare an Ippon if sufficient. And if that party has already scored an Ippon then the judge should call out Nihon and terminate the contest'.

Kano went on to say that when Waza-ari was called it should represent at least 60-70% of a full throw and he went on to discuss the various percentages that would be acceptable for subsequent scores (bearing in mind that the judge had the freedom to award a (cumulative) waza-ari score after more attempts. He suggested that if one near-miss was worth 70% of a full score then a subsequent score of 30% would be sufficient to call a Waza-ari if he had not done so on the first near-miss. Then of course there was the problem of how to evaluate three near-miss attacks each, of say 40%.

These uncodified musings were complicated but what is interesting is how early on the Butokukai rules, as first drafted by Kano, approached the logic of the koka (3 points), yuko (5 points), waza-ari (7 points) and ippon (10 points) scoring system introduced by the International Judo Federation in 1967.

With regard to the length of the contests the Butokukai rules stated that the judge should call the contest a draw (hiki-wake) if no scores had been made after a *suitable time* (Article 4). Kano explained that the length of the contest was up to the judge. If time was short and there were a lot of other people waiting to compete the judge could quickly terminate the contest and call hikiwake. If, on the other hand, there was more time he could allow them to carry on as long as necessary to test their skills. Even so the judge could terminate a match after a suitable time if two contestants were evenly matched. In a team competition in 1900 the contest time was fixed at 15 minutes, but the judges led by Tomita Tsunejiro still had discretion and allowed some contests to carry on for up to 42 minutes among the higher graded competitors.

Kano had this to say about the Butokukai rules created by the committee:

'Since so many people have gathered together to decide upon these rules I would like to use them as quickly as possible in the Kodokan. Although jujitsu and Kodokan judo were originally different the present-day jujitsu-ka have gradually changed their views in accordance with the changing times and approached many of the points that Kodokan judo stresses, therefore I feel we have managed a good compromise on the Butokukai Randori and Competition Rules. These rules are not something that I created for the Kodokan. They were created for the Butokukai and because they have been created with reference to present jujitsu masters I can see no problem in using them in the Kodokan, but believe it is preferable to use them in the light of the Kodokan objectives'.

The most glaring omission from these Butokukai Jujitsu rules was *Atemi* (kicks and punches) which according to Kano was one of the main techniques of the jujitsu of the time, along with groundwork. A possible reason for the exclusion might have been a practical one. Should they have allowed full knock-out blows or gone for the type of karate scoring where strikes had to be on target but pulled? On the other hand Kano was against anything that harmed the body as this would have gone against his physical education ideal.

Also, throws had pitch the opponent face up (supine), but many jujitsu throws were on to any part of the body such as face-down (prone), on to the head or shoulders or combined with a joint-lock.

Furthermore restraint techniques (*osae-waza*) were not defined in the rules. Many jujitsu restraint techniques were on prone opponents or on positions other than on the back. Allowing them would have significantly changed the nature of Kodokan judo groundwork. The only other definition/reference to restraints is in rule 11 which says that the judge can call an ippon if after a suitable amount of time the opponent *cannot rise to his feet*.

Jujitsu seems to have got a raw deal out of these rules, but since there were no rules on the battlefield the process of applying any sort of rules to jujitsu competition and randori inevitably turned it in the same direction as judo.

The Kodokan judo randori and competition rules

Within a very short space of time (i.e., by 1900), Kano adopted the Butokukai jujitsu rules for the Kodokan almost in their entirety but made them competition and randori rules. Of the 13 articles of the Butokukai rules Kano adopted ten without change but modified three articles (2, 12 & 13) in minor ways.

Article 2 of the new Kodokan rules was the same as the original Butokukai rule except that the following was added: 'However, in competitions below 1st Dan grade kansetsu-waza (joint-locks) are not included.'

The explanation of this was that those who had the training could moderate the application of their kansetsu techniques and distinguish between those who could endure them and those who could not. However, those in the early stages of their judo could do neither, which was dangerous. In particular, locks such as neck locks could cause irreversible damage, which made it necessary to restrict their use.

Article 12 was changed to read, 'For those below 1st Dan, throws and groundwork to a ratio of 70-80% throwing and 20-30% groundwork should be done in normal training. The ratio for those above 1st Dan is 60-70% throwing and 30-40% groundwork. However, if in competition one contestant should avoid fair methods and use base means to avoid either throwing or groundwork he should be cautioned by the judge and made to compete according to the recognised fair rules of the judge.'

Article 13 was changed to read – '1st Dan and above are not allowed to use toe and finger locks or ankle and wrist locks'.[76]

Thus emphasis was placed on throwing in the Kodokan Randori and Shiai rules. Kano justified this emphasis as follows:

'Throwing is good for the physical education of the body because it uses so many parts of the body and because the principles of throwing are more advanced. Also using katame-waza against multiple assailants does not work. When it is one-to-one a person can use shime-waza to

---

[76] Kano excludes wrist-locks here which were not excluded in the Butokukai rules possibly because of those jujitsu schools which did wristlocks such as the Aiki Jujitsu schools. As with the Butokukai rules he does not specifically exclude knee, shoulder, neck and spine locks.

strangle an assailant unconscious and then tie him up, but it takes time to kill someone with shime. In this case there is always the fear that a stronger person would use atemi-waza to free himself. If one moves nimbly when doing throws it is possible to take on many assailants. Furthermore if one trains fully at throwing it is easier to work on groundwork later but if one concentrates on groundwork to begin with it is difficult to switch to throwing later on. In the end it is best to practise both throwing and groundwork but to emphasise the throwing in the beginning. Beyond 1st Dan level the students can put his emphasis where he wishes'.

Kano was always firm on this distinction.

One noteworthy fact about these Butokukai and Kodokan judo rules is the absence of any reference to Kime-waza or decisive technique. The ippon throw is usually thought of as a real combat deciding technique, but clearly fighting for the best of three ippons sidesteps that definition. Kano said the competition and randori rules were to test the ability of the contestants in standing and groundwork.

Like the later establishment of the Butokukai kata (see below) the formulation of the Butokukai randori and competition rules was a coup for Kano. In many ways he was just the young head of an upstart jujitsu school (which is probably how the Butokukai first regarded Kodokan judo). However, because he was the sole academic on the committee, and had a flourishing dojo and no doubt because of his impeccable personal connections, he was entrusted with the job of drafting then preparing the rules.

It is clear that the Kano view prevailed. As one Yoshin-ryu jujitsu master later complained, 'We agreed to rules that deprived us of many of our techniques. It was like taking wings away from a bird'.

During the Pacific War the Butokukai made some attempt to add battlefield realism to the rules by mixing atemi with throws (see Chapter 16 – Wartime Judo), but the ending of the war prevented its introduction.

Later judo rule changes

The Kodokan rules were modified over the following years. Much of the modification up to the end of the Pacific War seemed to be a *repeat* of what was *not* allowed, which would indicate a certain amount of difficulty in eliminating these techniques. Prior to the 1941- 45 Pacific War the Japanese regulated the judo rules entirely by themselves, but after the war foreign influence gradually increased, to the point that certain changes such as weight categories and blue judo suits were brought in which the Japanese objected to but could not stop.

In the 1916 rule modifications it was stated that *dojime* (trunk/kidney squeeze), finger-locks, neck-locks and *ashigarami* were not allowed. Perhaps one can assume that the *ashigarami* leg-lock was used in competition and randori up to this point. Also, of course, *ashi-garami* is just one specific leg-lock technique so did that mean other leg and knee locks were allowed[77]? With the big increase in competitions, rules relating to the handling of injuries in contest were introduced as were rules relating to the violation of the judo spirit.

In 1925 stricter rules for the transition from standing to groundwork were brought in (see Chapter 12 – *Kosen* judo and groundwork). Groundwork had to result naturally from the flow of the contest such as from a standing throw attack. This was a reaction to the so-called Kosen judo which specialised in groundwork. See Chapter 12 – Superiority wins (Yusei-gachi). Disqualification was introduced for those who repeatedly wrapped both legs around the opponent's neck, putting the hands or feet directly on the opponent's face, using finger-locks to escape from strangles, using the belt or skirt of the jacket to bind the opponent's head or limbs and putting the foot inside the belt or jacket. Anything that endangered the spine or neck was banned, but the situation regarding various locks was finally clarified by banning all joint-locks other than the elbow–lock[78]. Other bans included lifting the opponent up from the mat and dropping him, continuing an arm-lock on an opponent who has lifted the attacker up from the mat, and inserting the fingers into the opponent's sleeve and trouser openings. At this time the rules were also amended to allow Superiority Wins (yuseigachi) based on the contestant's spirit, posture and attitude at the end of a drawn match. See Chapter 12 for more on this.

In 1941, just three years after Jigoro Kano's death, rules relating to movement off the mat (*jogai*) and for end of match decisions (*hantei*) were

---

[77] There is on record a squabble between two competing high schools in Japan when a judge disallowed a leg-lock. The protest against this was that the knee lock used was not an ashigarami!

[78] This was 43 years after the founding of the Kodokan!

introduced. With regard to groundwork specific bans, such as clinging to both legs in order to go into the ground, kneeling or lying on the back in order to invite groundwork, hanging onto one side of the jacket with both hands in order to force a draw, and pulling the opponent straight down into groundwork from the *Hajime* call were re(?)introduced. The urge to do nothing but groundwork seems to have been very strong and still is as can be seen with the growth of Brazilian jujitsu.

Looking at what was banned it would seem that judo was quite a rough sport up to this point, and that repeated bans on certain actions indicated the difficulty in eliminating them. Trevor Leggett (Kodokan contest 5th Dan) who trained in Japan just before the Second World War told the author that the judo was much rougher then. According to him it was common to grab the testicles when doing *te-guruma* hence its alternative name of *kintsukami* (ball grab).

Further rule revisions occurred in 1951, 1955, 1961, 1962 and 1967, paralleling the growing internationalisation of the sport, which staged its first world championships in 1956 and was included in the Olympic Games in 1964. This also paralleled the increasing influence of television on sport.

The early world championships had no weight categories and were really a competition to find the single strongest judoman in the world. This tradition of finding the single strongest man still continues today in Japan in the All Japan Championships, although championships fought in weight categories are now also common in Japan.

Major new regulations introduced over this period were: weight categories, smaller scores (*koka* etc), scoreboards, combination scores, a tiered penalty system, penalties for moving out of the contest area, loss-time, referees' wear and gestures, passivity penalties, repechage system etc. Later on, blue judogis were introduced so as to distinguish the contestants.

Apart from the Butokukai jujitsu and Kodokan judo rules there were also other sets of judo rules in Japan such as Imperial Household (*Kunaisho*) judo rules, the Tokyo Metropolitan Police (*Keishicho*) rules, the Imperial Universities Specialist High Schools (*Kosen*) rules and the judo rules for the Japanese soldiers in Korea and Manchuria. In most of these other sets of rules the main elements (ippon throw etc) were the same as those of the Kodokan, but there were differences in procedures and names. The Kosen rules allowed easy transition to groundwork up to about the

1990s. The Imperial Household rules were for those competitions held before the Emperor (*Tenran-shiai*) which had to look good, and at the Imperial Palace police dojo (*Saineikan*) in Tokyo.

The Butokukai ranking system

In 1902 the Butokukai established its ranking system. This was possibly as a result of the popularity of the Kodokan ranking system. The martial arts abilities and status of Butokukai members were recognised by the titles of Hanshi (professor), Kyoshi (teacher), Renshi (trainee) *and* the grades from 1st to 10th Dan. This was a departure from the old jujitsu ranking system of Inka (permission) and Menkyo (licence), and the progression from Hatsuden (beginning), Chuden (middle), Okuden (inner) to Menkyo Kaiden (full mastery). The jujitsu ranks were mostly awarded for mastery of increasingly difficult techniques as opposed to the Kodokan ranking system, which was awarded for beating stronger and stronger people in contest. The inclusion of the grades 1st to 10th dan suggests a blurring of the differences between jujitsu and judo and a movement towards the Kano view of things.

To qualify for the rank of Renshi a martial artist had to have participated in the Butoku-matsuri and the Dai-Enbu-Taikai competition and be qualified to take the examination, as selected by the judging council. A certificate of having passed the requisite hard training was also issued (*seiren-sho*).

To qualify for the rank of Kyoshi a martial artist must already have the rank of Renshi, be 5th Dan or above and be well-behaved with considerable knowledge of his martial art.

To qualify for the rank of Hanshi a martial artist must already have had the rank of Kyoshi for more than seven years or be above the age of 60, be virtuous and pure with mature technique and be a model for others in his chosen path.

In 1903 Totsuka Eibi of the Yoshin-ryu of jujitsu and Hoshino Kumon of the Shiten-ryu jujitsu both received the rank of *Judo-hanshi* and two years later, after a revision of the qualifications, the following jujitsu men received the title of Hanshi from Kano: Yano Hirotsugu (Takeuchi-ryu of Kumamoto), Eguchi Shozo (Kyushin-ryu of Kumamoto, Noda Kensaburo (of Okayama) and Sekiguchi Jushin (Sekiguchi-ryu of Wakayama). (See the later section on the Butokukai Kata and the committee of jujitsuka who formulated the kata. Many of the above who were made Judo-hanshi by Kano sat on that committee!)

This may have been an attempt by the Kodokan to muddy the waters by awarding its own rank of Hanshi and bringing on side a number of the existing jujitsu masters. Do not confuse this with the word Shihan. Both words mean master although the characters are slightly different. Kano Jigoro is usually referred to in Japanese judo books as the Shihan (master). This Butokukai ranking system was revised in 1918, and again in 1934 when the qualifications for Renshi were recast.

The establishment of the Butokukai Kata

In 1906 the Butokukai ordered all the martial arts and their various schools to work on their traditional kata in their home towns and then present them at the Butoku festival, so as to be able to establish and transmit them for the benefit of later generations. Kata as already noted were the chief training method of the Jujitsu schools. The Kata were set-piece (choreographed) sequences/drills of attack and defence where each side knows what the other will do. For safety and other reasons no deviation from the kata is allowed.

This was a significant moment for the jujitsu people who desired to have their kata recognised and established by the Butokukai. The then chairman of the Butokukai was Viscount Oura Kenmu, and he suggested to Kano that they meet and discuss the katas. At the meeting Kano mentioned that two jujitsuka, Totsuka Eibi and Hoshino Kumon, were also judoka of Hanshi rank, and suggested that a committee be formed of representatives of various jujitsu styles to study their various kata with a view to establishing the best as Butokukai kata. Fierce rivalry was expected.

A committee of 20 men was formed with Kano as its chairman. The committee consisted of:

Name	Rank	Area	Style	Position
Kano Jigoro	Shihan	Tokyo	Kodokan Judo	Chairman
Hoshino Kumon	Hanshi	Kumamoto	Shiten-ryu	Member
Totsuka Eibi	Hanshi	Chiba	Yoshin-ryu	,,
Yamashita Yoshiaki		Tokyo	Kodokan judo	,,
Yokoyama Sakujiro		Tokyo	Kodokan Judo	,,

Name	Rank	Area	Style	Position
Isogai Kazu		Kyoto	Butokukai	Member
Nagaoka Hidekazu		Kyoto	Butokukai	”
Sato Hoken		Kyoto	Butokukai	”
Yano Hirotsugu		Kumamoto	Takeuchi Santo-ryu	”
Eguchi Shozo		Kumamoto	Kyushin-ryu	”
Takeno Kataro		Okayama	Takeuchi-ryu	”
Imai Gyotaro		Okayama	Takeuchi-ryu	”
Oshima Hikosaburo		Hyogo	Takeuchi-ryu	”
Tanabe Mataemon		Hyogo	Fusen-ryu	”
Sekiguchi Jushin		Wakayama	Sekiguchi-ryu	”
Tsuki Shigeyoshi		Wakayama	Sekiguchi-ryu	”
Katayama Takayoshi		Kagawa	Takeuchi-ryu	”
Hiratsuka Katta		Kagawa	Yoshin-ryu	”
Kawano IchiNi		Fukuoka	Shinto Hokuso-ryu	”
Yoda Ichini		Fukui	Hyoshi-ryu	”
Inatsu Seiko		Hyogo	Miura-ryu	”

Deliberation on the kata commenced in July of that year. At that time it was learned that a descendant of the Miura-ryu of jujitsu, which was directly descended from the Chinese Chin Gen-pin and his Chuan-fa Chinese boxing (*kempo*) of the 17th Century, existed in Hyogo prefecture. This was investigated and as a result an ex-samurai by the name of Inatsu Seiko was invited to join the committee.

A quick look at this list shows that the Kodokan was well represented, as was the Takeuchi-ryu with about five representatives each. There were a couple of styles (Yoshin-ryu and Sekiguchi-ryu) with two representatives. Kano of course was a master of the Kito-ryu and Tenjinshinyo-ryu jujitsu and could speak for their kata if necessary.

Japan is a society where things are officially changed only when there is a consensus for change. This would usually be established beforehand by informal talks between the interested parties. Then a committee would be formed to *agree* the changes. The committee meeting would not usually be an opportunity for springing new ideas or plans. In this case it was not a situation where an established jujitsu kata was either to be accepted or rejected by the committee but one where the committee actually tinkered with the various katas presented to them so as to produce the best. This

Butokukai meeting was attempting to standardise and consolidate the kata.

Kano as committee chairman presented three drafts of kata that the Kodokan had already put into practice, namely the Nage no Kata, the Katame no Kata and the Shobu no Kata. The eventually agreed Nage no Kata consisted of 15 movements which was an increase on the original ten movement kata as practised in the Kodokan. Suggestions for improvement were made in committee and agreed, with this kata accepted in its entirety. The Katame no Kata was likewise increased from the original ten techniques to 15 and was agreed by the committee.

The Shobu no Kata was more problematic. Kano's proposal was based on the Kodokan Shobu no Kata (later called the Kime no Kata) and consisted of eight Idori kneeling techniques and twelve Tachiai standing techniques. However this was not accepted till some years later, probably because it was straying into jujitsu territory with little consensus among the masters. Isogai later described the work of this committee as follows.

'The Butokukai Kata legislation began on July 25th and lasted a week. The fierce debate began at 8am and continued to 10 or 11pm at night. The Butokuden where the committee met was a wooden building and there were strict restrictions on the use of lanterns because of the fire risk. However the committee was allowed, for the first time ever, to use many candles, which turned night into day. The various members of the committee brought their younger students to help demonstrate their kata and their demonstrations and discussions were heated, as you might expect, in their desire to have them accepted. Both Yamashita, who had recently returned from America, and Yokoyama were fierce in their promotion of the Kodokan kata, and Hiratsuka of the Yoshin-ryu performed all the 400 movements of his kata which made him ill.[79] When he returned to his home town he unfortunately passed away. Katayama who was skilful at Iai (sword drawing) was constantly full of praise for the valuable points of the other styles and there were even a few who criticised the usefulness of free-fighting (randori) saying that if kata alone was thoroughly

---

[79] This gives some idea of how many techniques there were in the kata of some jujitsu schools. Other accounts say that there were 303 techniques in the Yoshin-ryu.

practised the enemy could be responded to fully. As you would expect, with all the different viewpoints coming to decisions was not easy.'[80]

Later on the Nage no Kata and the Katame no kata were grouped under the heading of Randori no Kata and the Shobu no Kata's name was changed to Kime no Kata. With the approval of His Imperial Highness Prince Fushimi no Miya Sadaai (the Butokukai president) the Randori no Kata were announced under the title Dai Nippon Butokukai Judo no Randori no Kata (The Butokukai Judo Free-fighting Kata) and these were accepted in their entirety by the Kodokan. It is not known if the committee accepted other kata.

Despite the fact that the Butokukai Kata Committee could not agree on the Shobu no Kata (Kime no Kata) draft at that time, the Kodokan carried on using it as one of their katas. The Butokukai later went on to recognise the Kodokan's Ju no Kata, Itsutsu no Kata, Kime no kata and the Koshiki no Kata.

It is interesting to note the debate about the usefulness or otherwise of free-fighting and the stress that some put on kata alone. The manner in which the kata were practised could no doubt vary from martial art to martial art. In karate or kempo atemi-based styles, for example, there could be a progression from working on one's own to working with a partner, and their kata could be done with increasing complexity, concentration and vigour. Note also how many techniques there were in the Yoshin-ryu kata. The fact that the Kodokan's Kime no Kata was not then officially acknowledged perhaps shows where the real interest of some of the committee members lay, which was in battlefield combat or what they thought was combat. Kano was no doubt content that his two main kata got accepted by the Butokukai. This Butokukai kata seal of approval was probably more important to the jujitsu people than to the Kodokan which was already doing a lot more free-fighting than the jujitsu schools.

The Butokukai grew into a large organisation, holding competitions and awarding grades, but judo was firmly entrenched within it. Later on as the Pacific War approached the Butokukai grew increasingly more powerful. After the war the Butokukai was permanently dissolved by the Allies but the Kodokan, as a private body, was not. This caused a certain

---

[80] Butokukai Magazine May 1934.

amount of resentment in Japan especially among those who held Butokukai grades. This also left the Kodokan as the main source of judo grades in Japan which was only briefly threatened when the International Judo Federation under Dr. Matsumae began awarding grades[81].

In an article in the Kodokan Judo magazine (April 1932) Kano outlined the relationship between the Kodokan and the Butokukai:

'It is safe to say that the two organizations have the same objective but proceed from different standpoints. Both started with similar clear aims and purposes but the Kodokan has developed over the years especially in the direction of applying judo principles to people's real everyday life (*jisseikatsu*) such as in work, food, clothing, housing and social relations etc. The work of the Kodokan developed into the research and application of the Great Way of Judo. The start of the process is bujitsu and physical training on the mat. In the Kodokan these are partial objectives and not the be all and end all of it. The judo that is taught in both organizations is exactly the same and the teachers of judo in the Butokukai have mostly been Kodokan students. In the provincial branches of the Butokukai there have been instances of non-Kodokan judo being taught by non-Kodokan instructors but such people were rare.

One of the aims of the Butokukai is to embrace all the various martial arts and within a single one unite or standardise it. Some ask why the Butokukai only teaches Kodokan judo in its head dojo but there is no implication here that the Butokukai has excluded other jujitsu styles. The reality of the present day jujitsu styles which are united with judo is that even if some attempt were made to teach jujitsu there would be few students because jujitsu is unnecessary. This is not because the Butokukai rejected them but because it happened naturally. Because both Kendo and Kyudo (archery) are not united the Butokukai has not necessarily limited itself to any one style.

However there is one problem to be considered and that is both the Butokukai and the Kodokan issue Dan grades. Over this there is no agreement between the two bodies and I fear that a grave situation will arise. The Butokukai originally had the three ranks of Hanshi

---

[81] In fact the Keishicho awarded grades.

(master), Kyoshi (teacher) and Renshi (trainee) and the Kodokan had its 10 Dan grades and five Kyu grades which anyone could progress through. However quite early on the Butokukai adopted the 10 Dan grade system. Those who trained and taught in the Butokukai main dojo were Kodokan people and their grades were quite high. However the number of Butokukai trainees increased and the Kodokan allowed the Butokukai to award low Dan grades without reference to the Kodokan Deliberation Committee. Gradually the standard rose and the grades needed to go higher. In the meantime a 10 Dan grade system was set up for Kendo and judo in the Butokukai and promotions were decided by voting in the Butokukai Deliberation Committee. However for judo Dan grades, Kano who was a Butokukai counsellor, had the final say for promotions to 5th Dan and above.

One other problem arose. The Butokukai main dojo was situated in Kyoto and it tended to only give Dan grades to those who trained there but Butokukai people outside Kyoto did not think this strange. This conflict over the Dan grade system could be seen when Kodokan men came to train or compete in Butokukai events or to dojos in the provinces. There the Butokukai people showed indifference to the Kodokan graded men and paid no heed to the Kodokan Deliberation Committee people. Then gradually and unawares more and more reckless promotions occurred. I (Kano) tried to resolve the differences by suggesting that the Butokukai stick to its earlier ranking system and the Kodokan stick to its original dan grade system. However the Kodokan system was obviously popular and no agreement was reached. The net result of this was that the Kodokan system which had been achieved after a long hard struggle was threatened with destruction. My attitude was that the problem was small and could be solved by discussion. Apart from the Dan grading business there were no other problems between the two organizations.'

Chapter 10
Consolidation

The 24 year period from 1882 to 1906 can be regarded as the first major period of development of the Kodokan when the basic framework was put in place. The 27 year period from 1906, when the Shita-tomizaka-cho dojo was enlarged, to the building of the huge Suidobashi dojo in 1933 can be regarded as *the* great period of development. This period came to be known as the 2nd Shita-tomizaka-cho Era. The Kodokan stayed in the Suidobashi dojo from 1933 till 1958 and then after a massive fundraising and organisational effort, it moved into a huge dojo with over a 1000 mats in Kasuga-cho in Bunkyo ward in Tokyo where it still is to this day.

In the first period of development we saw the emerging green shoots of the Kodokan and the ways in which the organisation survived a succession of small dojos and Kano's various career changes and then two wars, which greatly enlarged the numbers of those doing judo as the Japanese became increasingly patriotic. Whether judo would have developed as strongly without the turbulence of these times is a moot point. Judo began to exceed its critical mass.

According to sumo records, sumo dojos flourished all over the country and there was hardly a village or town where sumo was not practised. In 1903 the whole of Japan was focused on the deciding tournament match between Ozeki ranked Umegatani and Hitachiyama, which Hitachiyama won. Shortly after this both men were promoted to Yokozuna (grand-champion). Following this period of popularity, the sumo headquarters (Kokugikan) were built in Tokyo in 1909. At this time sumo adopted the name *Kokugi* (the national art) to describe what it did. Perhaps it felt that it was being pressed by the growth of judo.

It is interesting that sumo flourished at this time. In the early history of judo we have seen the connection with sumo (*sumai*) and yet here, 1000 years later, sumo was obviously regarded by the people as having similar functions as judo and jujitsu. In the three-way connection between sumai, jujitsu and judo the first two arts will freely acknowledge the connection, but modern judo tends not to acknowledge its sumo roots.

The 2nd Shita-tomizaka-cho era and the 300-mat dojo

At the start of the Kodokan in 1882 the dojo was a mere eight mats in size. Immediately before 1906 the Shita–tomizaka–cho dojo was 100–mat size but when it was rebuilt in 1906–7 it leaped in size to 300 mats, equalling an area about 21m x 21m.

As for membership numbers it is estimated that by 1906 or thereabouts the Kodokan had signed up 10,000 direct members in Tokyo and over 70,000 indirect members outside, helped by a rise in patriotism among other factors.

The rebuilt Shita–tomizaka–cho dojo, which was completed in 1907, consisted of a 300-mat *Dai-dojo* (Great dojo) which included the Master's seat (*shihan-seki*), dan grade seats and spectator seats. The Completion Ceremony took place on March the 23rd. Kano gave a lecture, randori was performed, a promotion ceremony was held and jujitsu katas of various styles were performed. (Despite the much touted clash between the Kodokan and jujitsu, Kano tried to preserve jujitsu and frequently included displays of it in Kodokan ceremonies).

This second great developmental period of the Kodokan was overshadowed by many profound international events including the First World War, the Russian Revolution, the great Kanto earthquake of 1923 when 100,000 people died and half of Tokyo burned, the Great Depression of the early 1930s and the slow path towards the Second World War. This did not appear to dampen the Kodokan's growth since in 1933 it moved into the 500-mat Suidobashi dojo.

The Suidobashi 500-mat dojo

Such was the growth in students that even the Shita–tomizaka–cho dojo eventually became too small. In 1932 a corner of land belonging to the Tokyo Arsenal (i.e. the army) was found close by Suidobashi. Kano held talks with the Ministry and proposed construction of a new Kodokan on the land. The Ministry of Finance, architects and interested parties were consulted[82]. Financial help was sought from all over Japan and eventually

---

[82] Do not confuse this dojo, which was right by Suidobashi station, with the later Bunkyo-ku Kasuga-cho dojo which was a short walk up from the same station.

work on the new 500-mat dojo started in 1933. This coincided with the 50th anniversary of the Kodokan. The dojo was opened for training and administration in 1934. At this point the 73 year old Kano was a member of the Japanese House of Peers and leading an incredibly busy political life with many other duties and interests apart from judo[83].

Even in the new dojo the numbers continued to grow, with estimated new memberships up from about 7000 a year in 1936 to 18,000 per year in 1945. This may well have been due to the patriotism of the time. From the time of the defeat and occupation of Japan in 1945 numbers fell significantly for a few years as one would expect.

The Kasuga-cho 1000-mat dojo

Despite the drop in numbers following the Pacific War, new membership soon picked up to such an extent that by 1958 a new modern 1000-mat six-storey dojo had to be built in Bunkyo-ward, Kasuga-cho, where the Kodokan remains to this day.

One other thing helped swell the membership of the Kodokan: the rapidly increasing Japanese population. In 1872 the population was roughly 33 million but by about 1930 it had almost doubled and was still growing rapidly. Currently in 2008 it is about 120 million.

During this second growth period Kano began to build on his earlier foundations by continuing his research into judo, installing his teaching methods, clarifying his ideals, fostering instructors and planning the promotion and development of his art on a national scale. He was in effect creating an early national association far larger than any other similar organisation in Japan.

The Kodokan Foundation

Up to this point Kano had developed his dojos almost single-handed, although he had a solid body of exceptional men to support him (see the list of 10th Dans below). However, he came to the conclusion that he needed to place the Kodokan on a firmer legal foundation, not least because his educational work took him away from the Kodokan and Tokyo for fairly long periods[84]. Following the establishment of the

---

[83] He was elected to it in 1922.

[84] Note the direct reference to the increasing demands of education on Kano.

Kodokan Deliberation Council (*Shingi-kai*) in 1894, he turned the Kodokan into a Foundational Juridicial Person (*Zaidan Honin*) in 1909 with himself, Wakatsuki Reijiro (later Japanese Finance Minister and Prime Minister) and Yahagi Eizo as directors. Viscount Shibuzawa Ei-ichi (a big industrialist and financial conglomerate founder who set up Japan's first bank and trading company) and Kakinuma were managing directors[85]. Included in the Foundation were all the branch dojos except the Naval College dojo at Eta-jima and the Kyoto dojo. Kano himself donated 10,000 yen — a large sum of money in those times — towards the establishment of the Foundation which survives to this day.

Within the Kodokan a body called the Kodokan Judo Association (*Kodokan Judo-kai*) was set up to promote and develop judo. This involved the publication of the Judo Magazine and led on to the establishment of the Kodokan Dan-grade Association (*Kodokan Yudansha-kai*) and the important Kodokan Cultural Association (*Kodokan Bunka-kai*). For more on the Kodokan Bunka-kai see Chapter 11 – Kodokan Cultural Association.

Dan-grade associations (*Yudansha-kai*)

The need for something like a Dan-grade association became more urgent as the membership grew and spread all over Japan and abroad. Personal contact between Kano and the members became increasingly difficult. These associations had three main aims. The first was to facilitate organised contact with and between members wherever they were. The second was to promote research into judo's physical and mental aspects, and the third was to recommend for promotion those who qualified for it.

As a general rule the Kodokan aimed to have a Dan-grade Association in every prefecture in Japan and in some cases more than one branch where population numbers demanded it. The first one to be set up was the Tokyo branch in 1922. Gradually the yudansha-kai extended over the whole country. Next Kano set up a Central Dan-grade Association (*chuo yudansha-kai*) which he chaired. The aim of this central body was to unify all the Associations and speak for them nationally (NB. the Butokukai also set up its own Yudansha-kai).

---

[85] There is an expression in Japanese that someone has a wide face (*kao ga hiroi*). What it means is that the person is widely known and knows a lot of (influential) people. Most certainly Kano had an amazingly wide face.

The Dan and Kyu grade systems

Kodokan rules relating to the dan and kyu ranking systems were revised almost every decade up to about 1942, according to the changing circumstances of the time. In the early days Kano or the *Kancho* (head of the dojo) would first note the progress of students on the mat, and then, if the students were ready, propose their promotion to the Shingikai (Deliberation Council) which deliberated on the matter. If they agreed Kano or the Kan-cho confirmed it[86].

In more recent times wins in the Kodokan monthly contests and the biannual Red and White contests became the criteria for promotion, along with the separate demonstration of the kata. This later system was basically a simple one but it had built into it important quality controls. Ten ippon wins against one's own grade over a set period of time were required for promotion, but as the wins were being accumulated the person concerned was always matched against people with about the same number of wins as himself. However the system was softened slightly by allowing those who failed to make ten wins in the stipulated time to be considered for promotion after spending longer *active* time in grade[87]. If a judoka did well by beating six or more opponents in a row that instantly fulfilled the points and time requirements for promotion[88].

It is not clear how Kano fitted into his own system. The Illustrated Kodokan Judo which was published by the Kodokan in 1955 states that Kano had the rank of 12th Dan, shown by an extra wide white belt, although I have never seen any other reference to his rank or to the white belt. The monumental *Dai-Nippon Judo-Shi* published in 1939 (just after Kano's death) mentions that 10th Dans *and above* wear red belts, and in the Kano Chosaku-shu Kano talked about the qualifications for 11th and 12th Dans, although it seems that nobody was ever made higher than 10th Dan. Staying outside his grading system –if that was what he did – was probably the wisest thing for Kano, the founder of judo, to do.

According to the records the following Japanese judoka have been promoted to 10th Dan by the Kodokan to date:

---

[86] While he was alive Kano was the Kan-cho. After him others were appointed.
[87] In other words they carried on entering the monthly contests or Red & White ones.
[88] These were winner-stays-on contests (Kachinuki Shiai).

1st Yamashita Yoshiaki
2nd Isogai Hajime
3rd Nagaoka Hidekazu
4th Mifune Kyuzo
5th Iizuka Kunisaburo
6th Samura Kaichiro
7th Tabata Shotaro
8th Okano Kotaro
9th Shoriki Matsutaro
10th Nakano Shozo
11th Kurihara Tamio
12th Kotani Sumiyuki
13th Daigo Toshiro ⎫
13th Abe Ichiro ⎬ three promoted at the same time
13th Osawa Yoshimi ⎭

The competitive grading system grinds to a halt around 5th Dan, with the very occasional outstanding individual being graded to 6th Dan on fighting ability. Thereafter ability on the mat declines mainly because of the arithmetic and arthritis. If ten wins per grade are required it takes a huge amount of people to produce one sixth dan – at least in theory. Beyond that grades are awarded for exceptional service in teaching and to judo generally.

The grading system has caused some problems over the years in most judo-playing countries. Most people desire to have a high grade but not all have the ability. As an honest symbol of somebody's mat ability it has a very useful function. It helps produce teachers, protect novices and it gives worthwhile goals for those not in competitions. However by awarding grades of 6th dan and above for *services* to judo, Kano opened the way for these *service* grades lower down the ranks. Some judo organisations have even given Dan grades to non-judo people such as politicians in return for favours.

It might have served judo better if the grading system reflected mat ability only, with perhaps five kyu grades and five dan grades (ten grades in total). The system grinds to a halt around the 5th Dan level anyway since there are few people of the same grade to fight. With a lower ceiling of, say, 5th Dan there would be more people attaining the top grade and those who had ended with a respectable grade of 2nd or 3rd Dan might stay content with a level close to the top. The grading system has many advantages but it should reflect real ability and be consistent if it is to mean anything. Note that the Butokukai created its own much simpler ranking system during the Pacific War. It dropped the ten dan grades and substituted five *Tō* grades. See Chapter 16 for more on this.

The All-Japan Judo Championships

With the rapidly growing judo population in Japan, Korea and Manchuria many competitions were organised annually. The main competition was the All Japan Championships which began in 1930 and which has continued to this day apart from a seven year break during and after the Pacific War. The All Japan Judo Championships was first proposed by Kano[89]. It started in 1930 and was sponsored by the Kodokan and the Asahi newspaper. Competitors were divided into two categories, namely specialist and non–specialist, and then further divided by age[90]. In total there were eight catgegories. This ran for ten years during which time some famous names such as Kimura won their respective categories more than once. With the sudden plunge into war in 1941 the All Japan Championships was suspended till 1948.

Tenran-shiai

There were also a number of major competitions during this period which were performed in front of the Emperor (*Tenran-shiai*). Typical of these was the Tenran–shiai of the 1928 Enthronement Commemoration Budo Championships (Go Tairei Kinnen Tenran Budo Taikai).

This championship stirred up a considerable amount of interest in the Budo world. The judo event was held in the *Sainei-kan* within the Imperial Palace grounds in Tokyo and was strictly organised by the Imperial Palace Police[91]. Heading the organising committee was Prince Saionji (later

---

[89] Gunji Koizumi of the UK was strongly against individual championships and kept them at bay until 1968. He thought they would produce self-centred and conceited judo-ka. Before that all internal championships were team events. It was believed at the time that this was the Kodokan view but as we can see Kano promoted the All Japan Judo championships from 1930.

[90] Specialists meant the teachers of judo.

[91] I was invited by the Palace police to train at the Saineikan which I did regularly, but was unaware at the time of its significance. It was without doubt the most magnificent dojo I ever trained in.

Education Minister, Prime Minister, Privy Councillor etc). He was advised by Kano and Hongo Fusataro, who was the Chairman of the Butokukai.

As with the All-Japan championships players were divided into designated specialists (judo teachers) and non-specialists who were representatives of the prefectures. The players were divided into small groups by lot and fought each other to produce one winner per group. The winner of each group proceeded to the next group repeating the process. The rules were also amended (see Chapter 12 – Superiority wins) to produce a pleasing spectacle. Prince Saionji and others addressed all 160 competitors, teachers and other parties to encourage and explain. In the final of the non-specialist group Kihara beat Shimazaki and in the specialist group Kurihara beat Ushijima.

It is interesting to note how the Emperor endorsed this competition by his presence and how it was also used to introduce rule changes. Not only was the Emperor present but both the Butokukai and the Kodokan were part of the process. Whatever difficulties there were between the Butokukai and the Kodokan were ironed out by the Imperial presence. The increasing number of Tenran-shiai held during this period seems to represent an organisational effort to focus the national fighting spirit.

Chapter 11
Theoretical Principles of Judo

The earliest exposition by Kano of his ideas on judo's theoretical principles and values was made in a lecture to the Japanese Education Society in 1888. This was some six years after the founding of the Kodokan and his appointment as lecturer at the Gakushuin. It was also shortly after the Kodokan's move to the larger Fujimi-cho dojo. At this point Kano had acquired several years' judo and jujitsu teaching experience and his dojo was beginning to grow. He was only 28 years old at the time but was clearly finding his feet.

The Japanese Education Society Lecture
At the request of the Japanese Education Society in 1888, Jigoro Kano put on a lecture and display entitled 'A Summary of Judo and its Educational Value'. Enomoto Takeaki, who was the Minister of Education and Privy Councillor, the Italian Ambassador and many other VIPs attended. The lecture is remarkable in that it shows how clearly Kano's views about judo had developed by this early stage. There were some later refinements, but here Kano expounds the core of his teaching, firstly by contrasting jujitsu and judo. Kano's many observations on the contrasts between judo and jujitsu became a source of information about jujitsu which was otherwise not very well documented[92].

Jujitsu, explained Kano, was mainly a method of attack and defence with or without small weapons (knives etc) against an assailant similarly armed or unarmed. Its practice exercised the body but its physical education value and its mental training value were largely coincidental. Since its practice also required tactics and thought, it indirectly trained the mind and the valuable qualities of courage and calmness were also acquired.

---

[92] Kano probably had his own agenda but seems to have been quite balanced in his comments about jujitsu.

The methods of jujitsu training were divided into kata (choreographed sequences/drills) and randori (free-fighting) but there were many styles of jujitsu[93]. Some only did kata training while others did mostly kata and a little randori. The randori methods varied depending on the style. Generally speaking there were four sorts of jujitsu randori:

1. Mainly throws according to the rules and principles of the style
2. Mainly throws but using more strength than technique
3. Chiefly strangles and arm wrenches
4. Mainly restraining the opponent and limiting his freedom to move.

Jujitsu kata also had distinctive features. In terms of spiritual content, as opposed to physical, both Tenjinshinyo and Kito styles (which Kano had studied) were fine representatives of Japanese jujitsu and the product of a lot of thought. But times and people changed and some parts no longer applied to modern conditions. For example, among the Tenjinshinyo katas there are many moves done with swords but nowadays [when swords are not worn] it would be better to simply move behind the opponent. Many techniques are done with wide kimono sleeves but now many wear tighter Western style sleeves. Many of the techniques seem to have been included for appearance's sake and seem to miss the point, and since there are many strangles, arm-locks and wrenches a modern person might fear they go against the principles of physical education[94].

Although the Kito-ryu kata are the best and most elevated among the jujitsu kata, Kano wondered what advantage there would be to using them and whether they were appropriate as a physical training method, because firstly, the types of movement within them are limited, secondly, they take time to do, and lastly they are not appropriate for schools since too many facilities are required.

However, by making some improvements to jujitsu Kano thought it was possible to make it a good method of physical, intellectual and moral education, and after some years of thought, by selecting the good bits and

[93] According to the authoritative Nippon Budo Zenshu there were 179 recorded styles of jujitsu.

[94] Armlocks that were wrenched on in order to damage the joint were obviously against the principles of physical education but Kano went on to include armlocks and strangles in his system.

rejecting the bad bits of jujitsu Kano created Kodokan Judo with three objectives or purposes, namely: physical education (*taiiku-ho*), combat training (*shobu-ho*) and moral training (*shushin-ho*).

The combat purpose (*shobu-ho*) of Kodokan Judo he defined as 'the ability to physically control others and not be controlled by them'[95]. He wove throws, striking techniques and groundwork into his kata and considered how randori could be practised by those able to do it.

Since the purpose of physical education is to make the body healthy, strong, durable and mobile, Kano made certain changes to the original jujitsu kata and randori methods in order to shape Kodokan judo to this physical education ideal. First he removed all dangerous techniques and then re-formed what was left in such a way that all muscles would be worked in a uniform way. He contrived to make the training as useful as possible even where only one part of the body was worked. He then went on to consider various new kata.

As for the moral training purpose of judo Kano divided this into three strands:

1. Moral education (*toku-iku*)
2. Intellectual education (*chi-iku*)
3. Application of the principles of combat to the student's daily life (*shobu no riron no oyo*).

Kano believed that moral training would happen spontaneously from judo training and from instruction around facts stemming from the judo environment. He had a high expectation of the former, particularly in the acquisition of good etiquette before, during and after training, and the fostering of self control. The latter he thought was good for fostering patriotism and a noble brave spirit

As for the training of the intellect Kano believed in the strong influence of judo training on observation, memorisation, testing, imagination, language and the many relationships between these.

In the application of combat principles to daily life, Kano stressed the detailed knowledge of relationships between oneself and others in judo

---

[95] Kano elsewhere defined 'control' further by including the ability to kill and prevent oneself from being killed. It was not just self-defence.

Above: Oxford University v. Metropolitan Police jujitsu teams with Tani and Koizumi (centre row, 2nd and 4th from left), 1927.

THE PICCADILLY SCHOOL

OF

JU-JUTSU

Is Open Daily for the
Instruction of the Wonder-
ful Japanese Art of

SELF-DEFENCE

TO

Ladies & Gentlemen,

Under the Supervision
and Instruction of **Prof.**

S. K. Raku Uyenishi

The Acknowledged Premier Expert,

Assisted by Japanese and English Teachers.

"At Homes," "Garden Parties," and Gymnastic Displays attended on Reasonable Terms.

**Male and Female Teachers Supplied to Schools,
Colleges, Clubs, and Gymnasia on Short Notice.**

Provincial and Colonial Readers of this Book can continue their study of JU-JUTSU
by Post, if desired, by communicating as below.

ALL ENQUIRIES, &c., SHOULD BE ADDRESSED TO MANAGER,

31 GOLDEN SQUARE, PICCADILLY, W,

Above: An advertisement for Uyenishi's Piccadilly School of Ju-jutsu from Uyenishi's *Text Book of Ju-Jutsu as Practised in Japan*, 1906.

The Shihan

Nagaoka   Isogai   Yamashita

Mifune   Samura   Iizuka

Above: Kano the Master and six of his 'lions' who later became 10th Dans.

Above: Kano Jigoro in full dress uniform and decorations.

Above: Category winners of the 7th All Japan Championships of 1937. Third from the left is the great Kimura. This was an open-weight event.

Above: Third All Japan High School Championships 1954, Nikko.

combat which give great advantage off the mat. As an example, Kano described what happens when an opponent is about to attack. First the opponent must be evaluated in terms of physique, strength, technique and temperament and one's own similar characteristics must be compared. Next the immediate environment needs to be taken into consideration, and then a decision has to be made as to how to deal with the opponent. This process applies equally in business, politics and education, he said.

Kano also attached importance to the following verse as applied to the teaching of combat:

In victory be not proud of winning,
In defeat be not downcast,
When the going is easy be not careless
When the going is tough be not afraid
Just tread the Way

This he thought was vital in daily life, and of course in combat[96]. He paraphrased it thus, 'Whatever situation one is in exhaust the highest means to deal with it.'

Kano added:

'Education, whether to advance the nation or society, was required to impart knowledge to the citizens, to train them in mind and body and to transmit enlightenment to this generation and the next. As for the individual's independent happiness, current education was biased towards intellectual training and failed to produce men of character. Since Judo is a most appropriate form of physical and moral education, if it were put in the nation's education curriculum not only would it correct the defects noted above but would without doubt foster, spirit, bravery and patriotism and help place Japan among the leading nations of the world'.

With these words Kano ended his lecture in 1888 six years after founding the Kodokan in Eishoji temple.

---

[96] Provenance is not known.

Kano's research into his Kodokan judo carried on but it seems that what we now know as the significant parts and objectives of judo were formed during the period from roughly 1900 to 1916 when Kano reached 56 years old. Most of that which survives today in written form is contained in the magazines Judo, Sakko, Kokushi and Yuko no Katsudo (effective action) which from around 1915 carried Kano's many talks and lectures on judo. Kano also wrote the book Judo Kyohon (Judo Textbook) in 1931. This was for middle school students[97].

Western judoka who have read a book or two on judo will probably be aware of the judo principles of Seiryoku Zenyo and Jita Kyoei and can perhaps translate them into English, but some may feel them somewhat abstract and may be drawn more to the third aspect of Kano's theoretical principles, which is the Application of Contest or Combat Theory (to daily life or work).

With the establishment of the Kodokan Culture Association in 1922 Kano consolidated his ideas on judo's theoretical principles and put his heart and soul into spreading them. He spent years travelling the length and breadth of Japan preaching his philosophy despite a growing frailty – he was hospitalised a number of times – and perhaps what spurred him on was the worsening world situation at the time. Kano was in a unique situation and wielded huge influence in Japan in a way which is rarely mentioned in books on judo. Having been elected to the Japanese House of Peers in 1922 Kano sat in the very heart of government and had the ear of the most prominent people in Japan. In addition he headed a nationwide organisation of thousands of judoka and was a member of the International Olympic Committee with many contacts abroad. See Chapter 13 – Kano the Renaissance man and the section on Kano the aristocrat politician for more on this.

Seiryoku Zenyo and Seiryoku Saizen Katsuyo

On the technical side the principles of Ju (compliance), Kuzushi (Unbalancing), Shisei (posture), the six kata, randori, Kogi (lectures), Mondo (discussion), Gokyo (40 throws) and judo's three objectives (mental training, physical training and combat training) were formulated

---

[97] Do not confuse this with Judo Kyohan which was written by Yokoyama and Oshima (but revised by Kano) in 1925.

quite early on, but the over-riding moral and spiritual principles Seiryokuzenyo and Jitakyoei took longer to clarify and settle[98].

In the first Kodokan Judo magazine issue of January 1915, in reply to his own question 'What is judo?' Kano answered: *'Judo wa shinshin no chikara o mottomo yuko ni shiyo suru michi de aru'* which translates as: 'Judo is the Way of using the power of the mind and body most effectively.' He went on:

> 'Judo training through the practice of attack and defence trains the mind and body and the essence of the Way is acquired. Through this method the self is perfected and the individual is able to contribute to the world – the final objective of judo training.'

This definition of judo as 'the Way of using the mind and body most effectively' was later changed to the 'most moral (highest) practical application of mind and body' (*Seiryoku Saizen Katsuyo*). The difference between the two was the introduction of the word '*zen*' which was written with the character for 'good' in a moral sense (nothing to do with the Zen religion) and *katsuyo* meaning practical application. In the underlined parts of <u>Seiryoku Saizen Katsuyo</u> one can see the genesis of the present day Kodokan watchword of *Seiryoku Zenyo* (highest use of mind and body). However, Kano himself seems to have used the watchword *Seiryoku Saizen Katsuyo* rather more than *Seiryoku Zenyo*.

Kodokan Cultural Society

In 1922 Kano established the Kodokan Cultural Society (*Kodokan Bunka Kai*). In the Objectives of the Society he states, 'We resolve to contribute to the world by applying the fundamental principle of *Seiryoku Saizen Katsuyo* learned from the study of Kodokan judo over many years'. In the following proclamation he resolves on the Society's principles and tasks and sheds more light on his watchwords including *Jita-kyoei*:

> 'We take as our chief principle the achievement of the objectives of all humanity via *Seiryoku Saizen Katsuyo*. This Cultural Society is based on the following:

---

[98] Seishin is the much-used Japanese word for spirit. As an adjective it means spiritual but not necessarily in the religious sense. It is often best to translate seishin as the opposite of physical i.e. mental.

1. We expect each individual to train at making his body strong and healthy, cultivating himself morally and fulfilling an influential role in society
2. With regard to the nation we expect reverence for the constitution and Japan's history and in order to plan for its prosperity there should be no no slackening in implementing all necessary improvements
3. In society we expect the realization of a pervasive harmony where individuals or groups help and compromise with each other
4. In the world at large we expect all to strive for the mutual prosperity of mankind, abandonment of racial discrimination and the attainment of equal shares in [the fruits of] cultural improvements.

Essential points are:

1. Seiryoku (no) Saizen Katsuyo is the secret of self-perfection
2. Self-perfection is completed by aiding other perfections
3. Self-perfection is the basis of mankind's mutual prosperity'.

Note the mention here of the word 'self-perfection' exposes the possible influence of the English philosopher Herbert Spencer (1820 – 1903) who was very influential all over the world, including Japan, during his lifetime. He was an early evolutionist who coined the phrase 'the survival of the fittest'. In his writings he expounded the belief that evolution could explain most things from biology to ethics, psychology and sociology. He expressed an extreme form of individualism and utilitarianism. Spencer's philosophy tried to demonstrate that it was possible to believe in the ultimate perfection of humanity on the basis of advanced scientific conceptions such as biological evolution. The end point of the evolutionary process would be the creation of the perfect man in the perfect society.

'Self-perfection', however, is a concept with a long history in Western philosophy and religion dating back at least to Plato. Whether Kano was influenced by Spencer is difficult to say. His diaries which were written in English and which are held by the Kano family may give a clue to this.

Confucian influences are very strong in Kano's writings and lectures. Few Japanese would subscribe to Spencer's 'extreme individualism'. Kano, as you will notice later on in this chapter, describes 'group life (*dantai* seikatsu)' as good (*zen*) and anything that hinders that as bad (*aku*). As noted in Chapter 1 Confucian martial artists tended to be interested in *hito-zukuri* and *kuni-zukuri* (building the man and building the nation)[99]. Kano's use of the expression 'self-perfection' here could however just be generally descriptive with no Western philosophical background to it at all[100].

It seems more likely that Kano was most influenced by Confucianism and its concept of *kunshi* meaning the perfect man who was a combination of saint, scholar and gentleman whose function was act as a moral guide to society. Kunshi were expected to cultivate themselves morally, show filial piety and loyalty and cultivate humanity or benevolence. However like most people he perhaps consisted of a mix of unconscious influences both Eastern and Western.

Kano continued

The tasks of the Bunkai-kai are:

1. Publication of magazines and books
2. Holding lectures and classes in Tokyo and elsewhere
   a. Carrying out research investigations into the daily necessities such as food, clothing, shelter, social intercourse and the various problems that should promote the happiness of the people; and providing necessary facilities for this
   b. Researching the morals of the nation, its physical well being and hygiene. And setting up the necessary facilities for this.

Kano's view of the current bleak world situation no doubt urged him on in his work. He wrote as follows:

'In recent times as I try to understand the situation in the world at large, I note that international relations day by day become complicated and believe that unless countries work in concert in reconciliation, maintaining [Japan's] independence will become increasingly difficult.

---

[99] Confucianism was the social, political, philosophical and moral teaching of Confucius which mainly stressed the duties of the ruler and the ruled, parents and children and the relationships between the various groups in society such as husband and wife.

[100] Some Japanese commentators have watered this concept down somewhat and translated self-perfection (*jiko kansei*) as merely being of good character.

In consequence unless we try to make friends in the outside world I cannot expect this nation to flourish. When I ask myself the question 'how is the state of the nation today' do I not see ideologies without far reaching ideals causing confusion among the people, upper and lower classses swimming in luxury and addicted to idleness, land-owners confronting tenant farmers, capitalists colliding with workers and everywhere in society a struggle for fame, fortune and power? I am sure impartial readers will sympathise with the necessity of adapting to the situation in the world and saving our country as quickly as possible from these circumstances.'

The Dark Valley (*kurai tanima*)

The above oblique but brave critique of the state of the nation was written during very turbulent times, between the ending of the First World War and the great recession of 1929. Japan had by then annexed Korea and joined in the European and American expansionist movement in China. During the First World War when the European nations and others were prevented from directing their attentions to China, Japan made the so-called Twenty One Demands on China in 1915. A weak China was forced to accept most of the demands which effectively made her a vassal of Japan. Japan consolidated her political and economic position there. Anti-Japanese sentiment in China grew worse and reached a climax in 1919.

In the quotation we can also see direct reference to the struggle in Japan against communism and socialism, which Japan managed to avoid. The period from 1931, when the Japanese army and navy took over the government, to 1941 and the attack on the American fleet at Pearl Harbour, is known in Japan as the *kurai tanima* or dark valley. In 1933 Japan withdrew from the League of Nations over mounting criticism of its activities in south-east Asia and this eventually affected Japan's bid to host the 1940 Olympic Games in Tokyo and Sapporo.

Before this time the Meiji period (1868-1912) was one of massive social and economic change in Japan[101]. The Taisho period (1912-1925) marked a slightly more liberal turn as the pendulum swung briefly towards a renewed interest in the Western model such as that existing in France

---

[101] It is common in Japan to date the year according to the reign of the current emperor. So for example Kano Jigoro founded the Kodokan in the 15th year of Meiji (1882).

and the US. During this period Japan was run by the Genro (Elder Statesmen) and the Kizokuin (House of Peers), but as they grew older the younger fiery lower and middle-ranking army and naval officers gradually flexed their muscles. The pendulum then swung back with a vengeance to militarism and ultra-nationalism.

In 1932 there was the so-called May 15 Incident (*Go-ichigo Jiken*) when ultra-nationalists, with the help of 42 young army officers, attempted a military coup and assassinated the Prime Minister Inukai and several other prominent people. This rebellion, which aimed at strengthening fascism, resulted in the defeat of the political parties in the House of Representatives (*Shugiin*) and the formation of a coalition government. Just a few years later in 1936 was the so-called February 26 Incident (*Niniroku Jiken*), when young army officers attempted another coup and assassinated many of the top politicians and members of the imperial household. It has been suggested by some historians of this period that even the life of Emperor Hirohito was in danger . Following both coups ringleaders were executed or ordered to commit suicide, but the drift towards fascist alliances abroad (with Germany, Italy etc) in the context of a major war with foreign countries (the US and UK etc) was plain to see.

Up to the imposition of military rule those in Japan had a difficult path to tread between the militarist government of the right and the revolutionary tendencies on the left. Jigoro Kano, as a leader of a major martial arts organisation and councillor of the Butokukai, was linked thereby to the militarist camp but his educational views inclined him to the liberal West. Even as the militarists took over Kano was still able to influence affairs so that his judo survived more or less intact.

Jita Kyoei, Sojo Sojo, Yuko no Katsudo, Bunbu no Michi/Bunbu Ryodo

The putting into practice (actualisation) of the basic principles of judo in everyday life was emphasised from the very foundation of Kodokan judo, but with the founding of the Kodokan Cultural Society it became more positive and concrete. Kano emphasised this principle in his lectures and classes in different parts of the country and in the magazine *Sakko* (*Awakening*) where he clarified it in the fields of daily necessities (food, clothing, shelter etc), social relations, work and physical education. He strived to teach each positively with an appropriate specialist.

In order for the Cultural Association to achieve its principles in society Kano stressed the watchwords Sojo Sojo (mutual deference-mutual help) and Jita Kyoei (mutual welfare and benefit)[103]. The final principles of Kodokan judo crystallised into the two watchwords Seiryoku Zenyo and Jita Kyoei ('moral use of mind and body' and 'mutual welfare and benefit').

It is thought that this emphasis on Sojo Sojo and Jita Kyoei was based on Kano's original research and was also influenced by his educational observation trip to Europe in 1920-1921 just two years after the end of the 1st World War. After returning to Japan from this trip, in a lecture to the Kinyo-kai (Friday Society) entitled 'Japan's Internal and External Strategies', Kano stated that:

> 'On this trip I gathered material with which to consider Japan's future position in the world. Japan should promote cultural activities with other foreign countries by changing from its original exclusionist and self-interested trends. In other words for the purpose of friendly relations a give-and-take spirit was required. In order to win out in this give-and-take situation the nation is required to raise its efficiency in all areas. The decline in efficiency is one cause of conflict and for that reason internal conflict must be strongly avoided. As of now both government authority and the authority of old religious morality have both collapsed.'

One of the results of Kano's first educational research trip to Europe in 1889 was to confirm his life's direction into education and morality. In Japan he had been much impressed by the imposing Buddhist Higashi-Hongan-ji temple in Kyoto. In Europe he was keen to observe for the first time the power of organised church and religion (e.g. Catholicism), but having done so he decided that the churches were like hollow shells and that education and morality were the way ahead. Later on he wrote that religion or education were the two basic choices facing a young man.

Kano went on, 'In order to remedy these evils of the time the appropriate application of judo's main principle – the effective application of mind and body (*shinshin no chikara o yuko ni suru*) – to all areas of the nation's life is required[104].'

---

[103] The two *jo* in this watchword are written with different characters.
[104] From *Kano Sensei Den (Tales of Professor Kano)*.

Kano here emphasises effective–activism (*yuko katsudo shugi*) saying that in order to enlarge the effect of moral education it needed to be based on the morality of mutual benefit. This formulation happened in 1923 along with the formation of the Kodokan Cultural Society. In December of the same year, Kano made the following lecture at the influential Friday Society entitled *Jita Kyoei Seiryoku Saizen Katsuyo-ron* ('An Essay on Mutual Welfare and Benefit and the Highest Application of Mind and Body'):

'Let me tell you about the training precepts which we judoka should keep in mind at most times. Firstly Kodokan judo students should know the differences between judo and jujitsu. Old style jujitsu was divided into many different systems (*ryu*) and was a type of military training devised by their founders. Their mental or spiritual foundations were taught mostly as simple rules and regulations for the warrior class. However students must also know that Kodokan Judo teaches methods of attack and defence in the light of (modern) scientific principles which create a rational physical training method within the framework *Bunbu no Michi* (The Way of Peace and War). In total they combine to create a martial art, a physical education and a moral education method.

As for our method of training the first thing which I must explain is how the Way of the Pen and the Sword (Bunbu no michi) is to be taught. As I have frequently said the basic principle of judo is Seiryoku (no) Saizen Katsuyo (most virtuous practical application of mind and body). In other words, with *zen* (goodness) as our objective the mind/spirit (*sei*) and body/force (*ryoku*) must work in the most effective manner. In which case if you ask me what zen (goodness) is I have to say that it is something which helps develop and maintain group life (*dantai seikatsu*) and that which prevents it is bad (*aku*).

Since in our country the [Confucian] virtues of filial piety and loyalty (*chuko shingi*) have long been preached and have been a potent force for developing and maintaining group life this is zen (good) and that which opposes it is bad (aku)[106]. Therefore because this group life or social life is maintained and developed and achieved by Sojo Sojo and Jita Kyoei both principles are also zen (good). This is the

---

[106] In this sentence he strongly exposes his Confucian tendencies.

fundamental principle of judo. When this fundamental principle is applied to attack and defence both kata and randori materialise. When this is applied to improving the body it becomes physical education (*tai-iku*) and when it is applied to polishing intelligence and fostering virtue it becomes a moral culture method for fostering intelligence and virtue (*chitoku no shuyo-ho*). When the principle is applied to the myriad things that people do in society such as providing the daily necessities, socialising, work, business etc it becomes a method for social life. Thus today's judo does not end at being the simple practice of a martial art in the dojo. The practice of kata and randori in the dojo is nothing more than the application of judo principles to a martial art and to physical education recognising the appropriateness of the teaching principles in the many things that people do in society.

Having said that people may ask, 'why do most people advocate judo principles through the practise of kata and randori but not practise judo principles separately from kata and randori?[107]' To this I reply as follows. There are different paths to the summit of Mount Fuji. In the same way, judo principles can be understood by approaching them from a philosophical point of view or from a political or business point of view.

However I discovered judo through the practice of old style jujitsu in its kata and free-fighting and experienced its inner secrets. For that reason I have toiled along the same path even in teaching. I did this because I recognised the value of teaching people a martial art and physical education via kata or randori and because I would like many people to live a rational life through the application of the principles of kata and randori. This is the basic training method of judo which I founded.

However there are a number of people in the world who lead a social life following the principles of judo without noticing that it is actually judo that they are doing[108]. If the judo I preach becomes more widely understood in the world I believe that what was hitherto not

---

[107] In other words off the mat.

[108] Note that the ancient Han Chinese word *jou-tao* (Jap. judo) meant a compliant and yielding attitude not a martial art. Kano in some respects seems to have made the full circle.

regarded as judo will become known as judo and that the ordinary person will manage his social life more and more widely on judo instructional principles. Let all of you strive to create this opportunity in society by taking the lead[109].'

Ascetic training (Shugyō)

Kano never stopped emphasising learning from physical experience as distinct from reading about it. This springs from one other pervasive principle in judo and that is Shugyō. The Japanese are not especially aware of this as a stated principle but it is always there as part of the background, like light in a landscape painting. Shugyō or simply Gyō is their word for austere ascetic training[110]. It is similar to another word, shugyo meaning study. The only difference in pronunciation would be the longer u sound in the second word. Both are written with two sets of different characters. So if I said in Japanese that I studied judo in Japan or that I trained extremely hard at judo in Japan both sentences would be virtually indistinguishable. Shugyō/Gyō derives from the austere training of the kind done in Zen and other monasteries and this is how the Japanese approach judo and other forms of martial arts training. It springs, I believe, from the Buddhist belief that the notion of the self is an illusion and an obstruction that has to be crushed by extremely rigorous training. Then like the Phoenix the real self can arise from the ashes.

My sensei Leggett related to me how his Japanese teacher used to explain a technique to him only roughly and then say: Now you have the root and to complete the Way you have train ruthlessly crushing flesh and bone for a long time never forgetting that the basis of our tradition is mental training.

This attitude of austere training is common to most physical, artistic and mental arts in Japan. Japanese chess (shogi) players for example often play in unheated rooms at the coldest time of the year to train their spirit. In the Shugyo mentality marathons are good for the soul and 30 minute jogs are neither here nor there. The four years of grinding training that Japanese university judo students would have to endure would be a good example of this.

---

[109] From Judo Zasshi magazine 1935 in an article entitled 'Kagamibiraki Kunwa yori'
[110] The Illustrated Kodokan Judo (p. 19) mentions Gyo in passing.

Judo etiquette (*Rei*)

As will be clear so far Confucianism exerted a strong influence on Kodokan judo and on the nation as a whole. One phrase you will often hear in Japanese martial arts circles is *Budo wa Rei ni hajimaru Rei ni owaru* which translates as 'The Way of the Warrior (i.e. judo etc) begins and ends with Politeness (*Rei*)'. This does not simply mean that all judo encounters start and end with a bow, it means that judo itself is an expression of politeness. When you bow to your partner or teacher you are expressing respect. When you bow to the dojo you are either bowing to the dojo or to the gods of war (*bushin*) therein. The exact form of judo etiquette differs from dojo to dojo and has to be learned. This may depend on its physical layout such as where the place of honour (joseki/kamiza) and the entrance is.

Rei is one of the five Confucian cardinal virtues. The others are *nin* (benevolence), *gi* (justice), *chi* (wisdom) and *shin* (fidelity). *Rei* can be translated as etiquette, decorum, ritual, respect, deference, manners or civility. In addition *rei* means the physical act of bowing which starts and ends any judo encounter.

In the dojo the Japanese are sticklers for bowing, which must be done on entering and leaving the dojo and to one's training partner or teacher when learning or doing judo. The importance of bowing to the Japanese was well illustrated in the Tokyo Olympics of 1964 when Geesink of Holland beat Kaminaga of Japan with a 30 second hold-down in the final of the open category. When the referee raised his arm to signal his victory some of Geesink's coaches and team mates began to rush on to the mat. Geesink immediately waved them back and finished the match with a proper bow. In this moment of major defeat for the Japanese they were immensely pleased that Geesink had preserved the correct *Rei*.

Asian 'sport'

Asian 'sports' such as taekwondo and judo differ significantly from Western sports in that they often have strong moral and social foundations. Kodokan Judo for example tells us *why* we should do it in its three objectives. It is taken for granted that there should be a reason for doing it. Sport in East Asia is meant to be good for the individual and the nation and is not primarily intended to be frivolous entertainment for the individual or the masses. For example Japanese kendo, which has a huge following in Japan, sees no need to enter the Olympics. The top English footballer Gary Lineker who trained and coached in Japan for two seasons wrote how strict the discipline was in team training. Scoring goals was not the objective – training the character was.

One other aspect of Asian 'sport' is the importance placed on the recording and *naming* of things which is originally due to Chinese Confucian thought. Confucius taught that social disorder can stem from failure to call things by their proper names. Techniques and equipment have to be named correctly and the names are not lightly changed. Compare for example judo with Olympic wrestling. Judo has its kata, its gokyo, its designated techniques, its objectives, its principles and so on, whereas a quick look at wrestling soon shows no general agreement as to the naming of techniques. Indeed the core of wrestling, the pin, can also be called a fall! The average Westerner would probably say 'So what!', but the effect of this technical codification is to ensure technical precision and the longevity of the art. In the long run the Asian arts will probably survive while Western forms may disappear.

Chapter 12
Later Technical Development

Kodokan throws

According to both Kano and Isogai 10th Dan, the jujitsu of their time was mainly atemi and groundwork. As for effective standing work (throws) the Totsuka Yoshin-ryu did Osoto-gari and Ashibarai, the Tenjinshinyo-ryu did Tomoenage and the Kito-ryu did Yoko-sutemi. It seems the jujitsu schools had about one good throw per school[111]. This may be because jujitsu was largely taught in a situational way as a response to variety of attacks. If one throw covered a number of these situations what need was there to invent more throws?

Isogai wrote,

> 'If you ask me what were the chief throws in the Kodokan in the early foundation days I would say that Kano used the Tomoenage of the Tenjinshinyo-ryu and the Yokosutemi of the Kito-ryu since these were the two styles he studied before setting up his dojo, but he also used the Osotogari and Ashibarai of the Totsuka Yoshin-ryu and achieved a reputation for the use of Ukigoshi, Harai-goshi and Tsurikomigoshi which is a surprisingly wide range of techniques. I can only bow my head in respect when I think of how Kano approached and studied the techniques of the various jujitsu schools.'

Among the (contradictory) accounts of the match between the Kodokan and the Yoshinryu in 1885 at the Keishicho (Metropolitan Police) it was said that the Kodokan mainly won with small techniques such as Ashibarai, Kouchigari, Hizaguruma, O-uchigari, Kaeshi-waza. These precise small throws based on skillful timing, footwork and fine body movement (*taisabaki*) were a distinctive feature of Kodokan judo in its early days.

---

[111] From Judo Zasshi magazine of April 1941 in an article by Isogai entitled 'My Training Years' ('Genyaku Jidai'). Note that this was written some considerable time after the event.

The Yama-arashi of Saigo Shiro and the Harai-goshi of Yokoyama Sakujiro became famous some time later. 'Up to about 1892 my Seoinage and Osotogari which I struggled to learn appeared on the scene and then not long after Nagaoka's Yoko-sutemiwaza emerged strongly,' wrote Isogai.

In *Judo Kyohon*, Kano describes how he developed his Harai-goshi. Saigo Shiro, his number one student, was very quick at learning how to stop techniques and began doing that on Kano's Ukigoshi by slipping round his hips as he turned in for the throw. Kano soon adapted to avoid that by balancing on one leg and using his other leg to sweep into Saigo's thigh. Thus Harai-goshi was born.

Kano also wrote about a very strong fisherman student and friend called Fukushima Kenkichi who caused him some problems on the mat. Kano thought about him, did some research among Western physical education books and came up with Kata-guruma which features in wrestling as the Fireman's Lift (or Fireman's Carry). Another slightly differing account says that Kano discovered a book on Western wrestling in the Ueno library in the Seido (Confucian college) complex in Tokyo[112].

Big throws and the re-designed judogi

The turning point for the emergence of the bigger throws was when the judo suit was re-designed. After the establishment of the Butokukai kata in 1906 Kano re-designed the judo costume which thereafter greatly affected how judo was played. Hitherto the judogi jacket had wide short sleeves which reached only down to the elbow and the trousers were also very short only coming down to the knees. The skirt of the jacket was often very long.

Isogai 10th Dan explained the reasons for the judogi reform as follows:

'Theoretically the judogi should afford freedom of movement and should enable the thrower to throw wherever he takes a grip. However with the judogi used hitherto it might have been good for right and left variations if both sleeve openings were gathered up, but if that grip was persisted in it restricted the movement of the opponent's arms and was only good for defence. This allowed for no technical progress.

[112] From an article by Professor David Waterhouse of the University of Toronto in 1983 entitled 'Kano Jigoro and the Beginnings of the Judo Movement'. Also in *Kano Chosakushu* Vol. 3.

Furthermore because both elbows and knees stuck out it looked unsightly and there was danger of injury.'

About that time Western style clothing with its longer, narrower sleeves started to become fashionable in Japan and this was incorporated into the design of the judogi. The judo-gi sleeve was lengthened down to the wrist and made sufficiently wide to enable a grip to be taken anywhere on it and the trousers were lengthened down to three inches below the knees. The long skirt of the jacket was also shortened. The defects of the original judogi were removed and the good points of Western clothes were introduced to create the judogi used to this day.

(Note that from about the 1990s the collar and lapels of judo suits became thicker and thicker which restricted certain techniques. This was eventually changed in 2007 but a knowledge of judo history as above might have helped avoid the problem. Technique and the judo suit are intimately related.)

From the advent of the new judogi through to the Taisho era (1912-1925) the nimble smaller techniques scored less and less and the big techniques such as hanegoshi, uchimata, seoinage, harai-goshi became more popular and this was paralleled by a growing tendency to look down upon groundwork.

Isogai 10th Dan wrote:

'After the establishment of the new judogi the smaller techniques which the Kodokan was famous for gradually disappeared and one could see the change to big techniques. In particular because the Butokukai instructors concentrated on hip techniques they became very advanced in Uchimata, Hanegoshi and Seoinage. Around 1912 to 1915 – a period when this trend was most conspicuous – the generally accepted idea was that contest was standing techniques (*tachiwaza*) and that meant big throws and those who went into contest hoping to win on the ground were noisily abused.[113]'

Judo and wrestling

It is interesting to speculate on possible Western influences on judo. At the time when judo was emerging wrestling was also being ressurected

---

[113] Isogai, *My training Era* (*Genyaku Jidai*).

and placed in the first modern Olympics of 1896. This wrestling was supposed to be the same as that held in the ancient Olympic Games although it now appears this was not the case. Instead it was based on a type of wrestling which was called Greco-Roman that survived in the south of France (a former part of the Roman Empire).

It would seem likely that Kano would have been interested in observing the wrestling but whether he saw any of this wrestling in action on his first educational research trip to Europe in 1889-91 is not known. Baron Coubertin expounded on the importance of sport at the Paris exposition in 1889, which is when Kano was in France. After Kano became an IOC member in 1909 he must certainly have become aware of it. Greco-Roman wrestling was introduced first in 1896. Freestyle wrestling, which was based on the English catch-as-catch-can wrestling, was introduced in 1904. For many years these two styles were the only models of international wrestling Kano could look to although many countries had their own native style of wrestling. Note that the Kodokan rules were codified in 1900, the year in which the second of the modern Olympics was held.

From what we know of the present day two Olympic wrestling styles it would seem likely that technically, wrestling had little to offer judo, mainly because judo's use of the jacket, with its many grip positions, created a much wider offensive and defensive range of techniques[114]. However, the wrestling *rules* may have indirectly contributed to judo.

Winning in wrestling is by briefly pinning the opponent simultaneously on his two shoulders or shoulder blades. Throws in themselves do not score – they are merely a means to an end, namely taking the opponent down and into a pin[115]. However it is very rare for a wrestler to lose from a double shoulder pin as it is difficult to achieve. Getting one shoulder to the ground is not so difficult but when the second shoulder is pushed down the other one tends to pop up. So winning is

---

[114] For example a lot of grip strength is required to grip and control an opponent's bare wrist but holding the end of a sleeve close to the wrist is very effective defensively and of-fensively.

[115] The rules in FILA international wrestling changed in 2005 to include scoring for throws. A similar FILA development was the inclusion of submission-wrestling (locks and strangles) within its organisation. Wrestling began to copy judo.

mainly achieved by directing the opponent's back towards the mat for which points are awarded.

However jujitsu, the prototype of judo, had many effective *face-down* pins[116]. Judo did not follow this, which raises the question why? It may be that Kano regarded wrestling-style hold-downs/pins on the back as a visually neater solution. Whatever the reason, Kano took the judo pin one logical step forward and allowed a 30 second pin with the opponent *largely* on his back (actually aomuke or face up) as a winning score in judo. This was much more realistic than the quick double shoulder pin which seems more of a symbolic form of defeat.

The Kodokan judo rules, unlike the Olympic wrestling ones, awarded scores for throws, but since judo was a combat art the throws had to be done with impetus and force. However, the judo rules stipulated that the opponent had to land face-up (in other words on the back), whereas in jujitsu and sumo, throws on to any part of the body are permissable. Throws onto the back may have been stipulated for safety reasons in judo (although sumo wrestlers do not pick up that many injuries despite the hard clay surface they fight on) or simply because they look neater. So perhaps Kano got some ideas from wrestling.

Judo and sumo

We saw in the first chapter that Kumi-uchi sprang from Sumai and that jujitsu sprang from Kumi-uchi so it is not at all surprising that judo, which derives from jujitsu, has a number of sumo-like moves in it. There are more than 20 sumo techniques in the traditional *Shijuhatte* list of 48 techniques that are very similar to judo, and some of the names are very similar – for example *ipponzeoi, kubi-nage* and *sotogake* etc. Apart from the traditional Shijuhatte list of sumo techniques, modern sumo lists 82 techniques (*Kimarite*) and referees are said to know hundreds more. Since sumo is done almost naked there are theoretically fewer grips to be had, which in theory should limit technique. There are however quite a lot of powerful sumo techniques that are done from a belt grip. Some combine with armlocks and of course there are many throws that are done by simply holding the un-clothed body. There is no requirement in sumo to throw the opponent on his back, so many contestants land on their face

---

[116] Many modern police restraints are face-down ones and are very effective.

or front. This is forbidden in judo because it is said to be dangerous, although sumo rikishi seem to survive quite well despite the hard surface they fight on.

There is some reference to sumo in early judo literature. As related above Kano had problems with a sturdy student and eventually came up with *Kata-guruma* which he saw in a wrestling book. However before that he went to a local *Nidanme* ranked sumo wrestler for advice[117]. He was shown a number of sumo techniques which he tried but found nothing useful[118].

Kano went for a clothed style of wrestling to approximate to everyday street wear and wrestling/sumo went for a semi-naked style. From the combat point of view, which was a major factor in Kano's choice, this was logical but he ignored the fact that light summer clothing would not provide much of a grip for a lot of judo techniques. Note that some illustrations of early jujitsu show the jujitsu-ka virtually naked apart from a loincloth. A combination of sumo and judo would have covered this situation[119].

Weak groundwork

In groundwork the Kodokan did not have absolute superiority. From about 1895 when the Tokyo Metropolitan Police and the Butokukai Bujitsu Championships first began, it suffered on the ground at the hands of Tanabe Mataemon (*Fusen-ryu*), Imai and Oshima (*Takeuchi-ryu*) and others, making it imperative for the Kodokan to concentrate on groundwork. This was the starting point of the Kodokan's more intensive study of groundwork which in turn led to Nagaoka and Samura (both later 10th Dans) going to Kyoto to study the strong groundwork of the Kansai area. Despite the fact that groundwork was studied more intensely and the Kodokan became much stronger at it, Kano's attitude was that

[117] This corresponds to present day Makushita division which is about middle of the ranking system.

[118] Vol 3 of *Kano Chosakushu*.

[119] Others thought so too. The author has a book called *Judo no Kenkyu* (The Study of Judo) published in 1925 which contains a large amount of pure sumo technique. It states that the techniques are to be used when suitable equipment such as mats and kits are not available. It is written by Hayashi Kunitaro 4th Dan of the Osaka Butokukai and contains not a single mention of Kano and the Kodokan or his ideals.

judo was mainly a standing art and that those who wanted to drop straight into groundwork from the start should be curbed by the rules. On the battlefield it is necessary to stay on the feet when against multiple assailants, he said.

The study of technique advanced as one after another new techniques were developed. This followed hard on the heels of the revelation of the principles of kuzushi (balance breaking). One of the features of Japanese judo is that because so many people do it there are experts on all sorts of obscure techniques, and the students themselves advance the frontiers of technique. Kano, however, stuck firmly to his belief that throwing was more important for combat reasons and restricted access to groundwork. Groundwork, he said, was not that relevant when faced with more than one assailant[120].

The Gokyo revision

In 1895 Kano, along with high grades Yokoyama, Yamashita, Nagaoka and others, set up a research conference where the techniques of the Five Teachings (*Gokyo*) were laid down as follows:

1st Teaching
Hiza-guruma, Tsurikomi-ashi, Uki-goshi, Tai-otoshi, Osoto-gari, De-ashi-harai, Yoko-otoshi (seven techniques)
2nd Teaching
Sumi-gaeshi, Ko-soto-gari, Ogoshi, Koshi-guruma, Seoi-nage, Tomoe-nage, Tani-otoshi (seven techniques)
3rd Teaching
Okuri-ashi-harai, Harai-goshi, Ushiro-goshi, Ura-nage, Uchi-mata, Obi-otoshi, Hane-goshi (seven techniques)
4th Teaching
Uki-otoshi, Uki-waza, Daki-wakare, Kata-guruma, Hikkomi-gaeshi, Tsuri-goshi, Soto-makikomi, Utsuri-goshi, Osoto-otoshi, Tawara-gaeshi (ten techniques)

---

[120] A very large student who worked as doorman at a night club once told me that he threw a troublemaker, put him in a hold-down and told him to behave. At that point he suddenly realised a soldid ring of people standing close around him. Anyone of them, he said, could have kicked him in the head so he got to his feet very quickly.

5th Teaching

Yoko-guruma, Yoko-wakare, Uchi-makikomi, Ko-uchi-gari, Ashi-guruma, Harai-tsurikomi-ashi, Seoi-otoshi, Yama-arashi, Osoto-guruma, Yoko-gake (ten techniques; 41 techniques in total)

The Gokyo was later revised in 1920 when its number was reduced to 40 techniques. The main changes that were brought in were the dropping of Obi-otoshi, Osoto-otoshi, Hikkomi-gaeshi, Daki-wakare, Tawara-gaeshi, Seoi-otoshi, Yama-arashi (seven techniques) and the introduction of Kosoto-gake, Harai-tsurikomi-ashi, O-guruma, Hane-makikomi, Sukui-nage and Tani-otoshi (six techniques).

Curiously a groundwork Gokyo was never devised, despite the fact that there is a lot of technique in groundwork. During Kano's lifetime the six kata and the Gokyo were his summary of judo technique as practised in the Kodokan. Kano's death in 1938 complicated the situation somewhat since nobody then had the authority to change the existing kata, create new ones or change the Gokyo. However the Kodokan went on to create the Goshinjitsu in 1956 which was in fact, if not in name, a modernised combat kata. It also created a list of Designated Techniques (*Shitei-waza*) in 1982 which with subsequent revisions now consists of 96 techniques (67 throws and 29 groundwork techniques)[121].

Bearing in mind the small number of throwing techniques practised by Meiji period jujitsu schools, this Kodokan Gokyo has an amazingly wide selection of throws.

Kano left his judo somewhat open ended. Although the free-fighting and competition rules restricted the judo for safety reasons, he included striking techniques (*atemi*) and locks (*kansetsu-waza*) of all sorts, *within his overall system*, particularly in the kata, but they were a limited selection. It might have been better if he had created extra kata with more of these techniques in them to round off the whole system.

For example there is only one leg-lock in the katas but in fact there are many other leg- and ankle-locks. The non-randori techniques in the kata are mostly put in a situational context where the opponent makes a

---

[121] In the 1960s there was a spectacular Gonosen no Kata which was a kata of counter-throws often done in slow motion. It was never clear whether this was official or not and it does not appear to have survived. It may have been a French invention.

particular attack and it is dealt with. The Kime no Kata covers most of the main attack situations but not the wide variety of techniques that could provide answers.

Early contest statistics

In the 1929 Tenran Shiai 123 matches were held, of which 90 were won by throws and 33 were won on the ground.

The throws that scored were:

Tsurikomi ashi	15
Harai–goshi	12
Osoto–gari	11
Seoinage	10
Uchi–mata	6
Kosoto–gari	6
Hane–goshi	4
O–uchi–gari	4
Ko–uchi–gari	4
Okuri–ashi–barai	3
Maki–komi	3
Tomoe–nage	3
Kaeshi–nage	3
Te–waza	2
Four other throws	1 each etc

Groundwork

Osae–waza	21
Shime–waza	5
Kansetsu–waza	7

As can be seen, the matches were overwhelmingly won by throws to a ratio of 2 to 1 over groundwork. Compare this with the modern ratio of 9 to 1. Also of interest is the highest scoring Tsurikomi-ashi (a 'small throw') which was immediately followed by four of the 'big throws'. Tsurikomiashi would not place very high in the statistics nowadays. Other than that the list of throws is familiar to most modern judoka.

Kosen judo and the restriction groundwork

Despite the Kodokan tendency to favour throwing techniques, the specialist high schools (*Kosen*) under the auspices of Kyoto Imperial University continued to concentrate mainly on groundwork and became very strong at it. In 1914 the specialist high schools held their championships for the first time. What they asserted was the right to go into groundwork in any way at any time and stay on the ground for as long as they wished. Since groundwork ability is almost directly proportional to the amount of time spent doing it those who spend more time on the ground will tend to beat those who do not, especially if the groundwork fighter is able, under the rules, to cling on the whole time[122].

At first the Kosen groundwork was positive and aggressive but some Kosen people began to show a tendency to change to negative, defensive groundwork in order to force a draw (especially in the many team contests held at the time). The Kodokan tried to remedy this by stating that:

1. From a martial arts point of view the standing posture is the freest for attacking movement
2. The process of combat is to start standing then to progress to the ground
3. From the point of view of physical development standing work should be emphasised during the early formative years.

But the *Kosen* people insisted that since the Kodokan and Butokukai rules clearly stated that judo contests include standing and groundwork that it was up to the contestants to choose how they fought. In order to correct this the Kodokan in 1924 first suggested changing the rules to restrict the transition to groundwork from standing. In the same year the Butokukai introduced similar restrictions on a trial basis in its Butoku Festival and Championships with favourable results. After one year of research into the new rules the following rule changes were accepted in 1925:

1. Article 1 of the rules to read – When running competitions in the Kodokan the match will be decided by standing work (nage-waza)

---

[122] A sensei once advised me that if I needed to make *rapid* progress before a major event to concentrate on ne-waza or counter throws

or groundwork (katame-waza); nage-waza includes tachi-waza and sutemi-waza, katame-waza includes shime-waza, osae-waza and kansetsu-waza

2. Article 2 to read – In competition, emphasis is to be placed on standing work and ground-work should be restricted as follows:
   a. When an applied technique gains more than half of an ippon but not a full one the contest can continue on the ground
   b. Groundwork may follow if either contestant stumbles when a throw is attempted.

Kōsen judo initially started with the No. 4 and No. 6 Specialist High Schools specialising in groundwork in training. Three things were noteworthy about their groundwork theory: firstly the likening of groundwork to the movement of water, secondly the very supple combined use of arms and legs and thirdly the way they fought in a ball when underneath on the ground.

Good newaza, said the Kōsen people, was like the principles of water, which had the following five features:

1. Water in whatever form does not directly oppose
2. When water goes underground it is not conspicuous but is the root of all things
3. Water flows combining pure with impure
4. Sometimes it is quiet at other times it is like the roaring waves
5. It does not oppose Principle (*Ri*) but returns to the flow of its own accord.

In other words good groundwork, like water, should seep, penetrate, infiltrate, combine and go with the flow. If it meets an obstacle it should go round, under or over it.

The No. 6 High School people also devised a number of supplementary exercises to create very supple joints and were able to work the arms and legs together in ways not seen previously. This was where the many later Sankaku techniques sprang from, and other locks and strangles.

The third feature of *Kosen* judo was the ball-like shape judoka got into on the ground, especially when underneath. This shape was used with great effect for defence and to roll and turn the opponent. In Japanese the instruction was *Shita ni nattara dango ni nare* meaning 'when underneath become like a round dumpling'[123].This was said to mimic an animal which rolls into a protective ball when attacked[124].

Despite the restrictions on entry to groundwork the *Kosen* people went their own way, continuing to stress groundwork for many decades after. They were, however, outside mainstream judo.

Superiority wins (*Yusei-gachi*)

The contest format by this time had settled down to one-ippon contests (*ippon shobu*) and if there were no scores, or if there were equal scores of waza-ari a draw was called. However with two strong evenly matched contestants it often happened that one or both might adopt excessively defensive and negative tactics and fight for a tactical draw, especially in team contests (of which there were many) such as between student groups or between geographical parts of the country. Some of the contest results that survive from this period show a preponderance of drawn matches.

In order to stop these often messy contests the Kodokan experimented with deciding the contest not only on the actual scores but on the contestants' *posture* and *attitude* as well. This took shape at the 1929 Tenran-shiai held under the auspices of the Imperial Household Agency which had its own judo rules. In these rules it was laid down that:

1. Judo randori and shiai will be fought mainly on the basis of standing work (throws) and ground work and in the event of a draw the final decision on the match will also take into account posture, attitude and technique
2. The refereeing team will consist of three persons, one of whom will act as a representative of the three and issue cautions and directions to the contestants
3. Decisions by the three-man refereeing team will be made on the basis of a majority decision and in accordance with Article 1 after having stopped the contest at the end of time.

---

[123] I trained regularly at the Keishicho dojo which was famous for its groundwork. Against two groundwork sensei called Shibayama and Miura whom I regularly fought over a four year period I only took a couple of ippons from each. Phenomenal!

[124] See *Judo Shiai Shimpan Kitei* (*Judo Contest Rules*) by Morishita and Murayama.

Based on the attitude, posture and spirit of the contestants the refereeing team could then award at the end of a contest a superiority-win (Yusei-gachi) to one or other of the contestants when their scores were level.

This implementation of the Yusei-gachi superiority rules in the 1929 competition that was held before the Emperor had one important result, which was a movement away from the principle of the clean ippon score. In the early 1920s Kano probably thought that judo was heading down a one-way street of groundwork-only judo. Not only did it look messy but it went against his ideas of physical education. So what better occasion to tidy it up than a major competition before the Emperor, fought under the new rules. It would have been difficult for the groundwork advocates to argue against a 'tidy' judo competition with the Emperor present.

These new rules which created the superiority-win were also adopted for use from the first All-Japan Championships (1930) onwards. Article 5 of the same rules stated:

5. When a contest could not be decided on the basis of Nage-waza and Katame-waza (i.e. when there were no scores or when both had the same results) it would be decided on the basis of the superiority of posture, attitude, technique and other movements of the two contestants.

Article 11 stated that when a match could not be decided on the above basis, having taken into account all factors, a drawn match (Hiki-wake) could be called.

The above rule changes were felt to have been successful in correcting the negative, defensive and unsightly judo which was the result of fighting for a draw and that they had put judo back on the correct path.

However the referees had a problem, which was how to evaluate any throw attempt which was worth less than a waza-ari compared with nice clean upright attacking judo, which looked good but might have actually achieved nothing at all by way of a score.

This sowed the seeds of the much later small scores such as the koka or kinsa (3-points) and yuko or waza-ari-ni chikai-waza(5-points), when the 'logical' Europeans said, if you are going to take into account these other considerations then put them on a scoreboard for all to see. This was after analysis of filmed contests showed that the Yusei-gachi decision did not always match up with what had actually happened in a contest.

In principle the Kodokan approved of the early Yusei-gachi rule changes but reserved its position by stating that the Kodokan should always strive to produce clean ippons in training, randori and shiai and that it should be wary of falling into easy matches where only a few minor techniques decided the outcome (as happens in present-day judo with Koka wins or low scoring passivity penalties). It also stated that if these small wins appeared, further research into the rules would be required.

Seiryoku Zenyo Kokumin Taiiku

On the kata front there was one development in 1927 and that was the establishment of the so-called Attack and Defence Style of the People's Physical Education (*Kobo-shiki Kokumin Tai-iku*) which later became known as the People's Physical Education (based on the principles) of Seiryoku Zenyo – (Seiryoku Zenyo Kokumin Tai-iku). At first glance this 'kata' looks like a karate kata in that it is largely composed of striking techniques (atemi).

The sequence is divided into two parts – 28 solo moves in the first part and ten partnered moves in the second. The second part which consists of five standing moves and five kneeling ones has significantly reduced atemi content compared with the first part. It includes for example wrist releases (*te-hodoki*) and defences against a sword.

There is a handful of atemi techniques in the other Kodokan katas such as the Kime no kata and Ju no kata but many of the counter moves in these kata use a throw or lock in response to the attack, not an atemi strike.

This Seiryoku Zenyo Kokumin Tai-iku 'kata' is a combination of physical exercise and atemi which is infrequently performed or used in Japan. Judo randori affords ample exercise for the whole body so one wonders what need there was to create this 'People's Physical Education kata'. Perhaps Kano felt forced to produce something incorporating atemi as a response to the militaristic pressures of the time, or maybe he wanted to keep atemi in his judo system for sentimental reasons since it was part of the Tenjinshinyo jujitsu style of which he was a master.

In Kano's book Judo Kyohon (1931) the Kokumin Taiiku sequence is illustrated but the blows show little focus, the stances are not convincing and there is little in the way of blocks, parries and counter attacks as you would expect to find in kempo (chuan-fa) or karate kata, for example[125]. It is a fairly static, linear kata (front~back~left~right~oblique) containing some moves which repeat and many of which look ineffective as combat techniques (for example there is one move where the demonstrator jumps up and punches with both arms above his head or from a standing position goes into a squat and punches the mat on both sides).

This sequence was not labelled *kata* and yet it was done as a set pattern of movements. However there was one difference and that was the sequence could be speeded up and repeated so as to create a workout. To quote the Kodokan, 'This was based on offensive and defensive judo techniques with reference to biology, anatomy, hygiene and pathology.'

Atemi

In Judo Kyohon, Kano clearly stated his technical schema which was a tripod consisting of tachiwaza (throws), katame-waza (locks, strangles and restraints) and atemi-waza (literally striking (*ate*) the body (*mi*) techniques) but little of atemi emerges even in the Kodokan kata[126]. In 1927 Kano said in one of his lectures to his students that he was looking at ways to incorporate atemi into randori but nothing came of it.

Clearly, striking, as a method of combat, goes back into the mists of time. An early development was the emphasis on striking the vital nerve spots, which was influenced by ancient Chinese medicine. For example, most of the vital spots (*kyusho*) of atemi correspond to acupuncture and moxibustion points. The names, number and functional interpretations of the kyusho differ among the various schools of jujitsu, of which few gave explanatory diagrams. The kyusho were mostly passed down from generation to generation by word of mouth.

A later classification by Japanese jujitsu was into instant-death (*sokushi*) and instant knock-down kyusho (*sokuto*). The spots of instant-death are anatomically closely related to the viscera of the brain and are mostly

---

[125] In the Preface Kano says that he had long thought about writing a book but had been too busy. However when judo was placed in the middle school curriculum by the Ministry of Education he thought it appropriate to produce something for middle school students in two volumes (*Jo* and *Ge*).

[126] For a fuller treatment of Atemi waza see *Kodokan Judo Kagaku Kenkyukai* bulletins and *Judo Koza* Vol. 3.

located along the median line of the body. The instant knock-down spots are mostly found in the extremities where the motor nerves run close to the surface and are usually the same on each side of the body. A strong impact on the former can lead to death and temporary damage to the underlying nerves on the latter. There is even one atemi strike known as *Ichiji nemuri- mikka koroshi* meaning 'temporary sleep – third day kill'. This may be the origin of the so-called delayed death touch.

The average number of vital spots per Japanese jujitsu school is about forty of which about half were instant-death ones[127]. Judo Kyohon lists only 12 vital spots which do not sound very many but compare that with the even fewer targets of boxing. Some vital spots are more difficult to hit than others and many are quite small and would require a hard, pointed part of the attacker's body (hardened knuckles etc) to strike with.

In jujitsu, atemi was used before, during or after other techniques. Apart from causing pain, loss of consciousness or death the other uses of atemi were to unbalance or distract the opponent before applying throws etc. A jujitsu expert would perhaps use his hardened knuckles to strike his opponent between the eyes, take a grip which pinched a nerve, wrench on a wrist- or arm-lock, throw him down to the ground and follow up with either a strangle or another atemi strike to a vital spot. Atemi seems to have followed karate's One Strike = One Kill principle as opposed to that of boxing with its blitzkrieg of punches and war of attrition.

Judo as we know was formed from two jujitsu styles one of which, the Tenjinshinyo style, specialised in atemi and restraint techniques. The atemi spots of the Tenjinshinyo style numbered 30. The other style which was the Kito-ryu specialized in throwing as its name suggests, (Ki = rising and To = falling).

It would seem that Kano had a problem with fitting atemi into his system. Quite early on he stated that atemi went against the principle of physical education in that its purpose was to damage the opponent's body, and he wrote it out of the competition and randori rules as a scoring method. However in his Judo Kyohon he also goes on to list, but not illustrate, 22 basic strikes of atemi which differ somewhat from the Kokumin Tai-iku sequence and appear more realistic. Kano writes at one point that the attacker should focus on the part of his body that makes the

---

[127] Spots found on both sides of the body count only as one.

strike, and some of the moves in the Kokumin Tai-iku sequence are illustrated with an initial step closer for more power.

At one point in judo's history the decision was made to incorporate atemi with randori. This was not done by the Kodokan but by the wartime Butokukai which had taken overall control of judo during the Pacific War. See Chapter 16 for more details.

Perhaps the nearest to a realistic mix of atemi and judo that we have seen in more modern times is the Ultimate Fighting Championships (UFC) cage-fighting. Here martial artists are matched against each other. Biting and gouging are not allowed but virtually everything else is[128]. Matches were won by submission or knockout and carried on for as long as it took. In the beginning the grapplers, mainly in the shape of Gracie Jujitsu won with their armlocks, strangles and some atemi[129]. Matches were mostly on the ground and often very long and some might say boring. However the strikers from boxing and karate etc eventually learned to avoid certain groundwork situations and the grapplers learned to use their fists and feet for striking. Things then got more complicated with a variety of other no-holds-barred formats, the imposition of rules and the inevitable drift to phoney pro-wrestling type competitions.

Note that sumo has a halfway stage for those grapplers not inclined to punch, which is to incorporate open-handed slapping and thrusting to the head, face, throat and neck. In a sumo stable the hands are hardened by slapping of the *teppo* pole. Clenched fists are not allowed in sumo nor kicks although sumo slaps can knock the opponent down or out. This accustoms them to attacks to the face and head. Incidentally in an account of one major judo match in Japan in the 1920s one contestant did sumo *hatakikomi* (slap-downs) on his opponent. Apart from the rule which bans touching the face, slap-downs do not seem to be specifically banned by the judo rules.

---

[128] Many of the *jujigatame* type armlocks which the Gracie fighters won with could easily be stopped by biting the leg as it comes near the face. I once saw the great Geesink give up on *jujitgatame* after his leg was bitten!

[129] It is said that the first Gracie studied with a Kodokan 4th Dan by the name of Maeda Mitsuyo who first travelled to Europe about 1905 to take on boxers and wrestlers and then went to South America and eventually Brazil. Maeda is said to have been a graduate of Waseda University judo club but may possibly have come first from the Fusen-ryu style of jujitsu as did Yukio Tani who accompanied Maeda on his trip to Europe.

Chapter 13
Kano the Renaissance man

It would be easy for judo people to assume that Kano did little else other than run his dojos and promote his ever growing judo organisation, but in fact he was incredibly busy with his other work and interests.

Kano the educationalist

At a very early age Kano showed his passion for teaching and education. Before he went up to Tokyo University he taught the four Chinese classics (Shisho) to local youths in Mikage and even at university he assisted the junior students with their studies. Up to the age of 22 he studied hard, eventually graduating from the top Imperial Tokyo University. Then he became a lecturer and administrator at the Gakushuin (Peers College) which catered for the children of the aristocracy. After that he headed the Tokyo Teacher Training College for 27 years.

Some of the aristocrat students at the Gakushuin were arrogant youths who despised the teachers, some of whom tended to be over respectful to their students. Many of the students plainly expected the teachers to run around for them. Most of the students were of clan warrior stock (*Banshi*) and even among themselves there was snobbery regarding the size and influence of the clan to which they belonged. Kano was not of Banshi stock and did not think of himself as one. Tachibana, one early head of the Gakushuin, was from a small clan and he tended to be over respectful to those from bigger clans. The next head, Tani, distinguished himself in the period up to the Restoration and was a confidant of the Emperor Meiji. Tani became part of the Ito Hirobumi cabinet and served as Minister of Agriculture. Later on Kano clashed with a Gakushuin head called Miura Goro who was a Lieutenant General in the army and a Viscount. Before working in the Gakushuin Miura served as head of the Army College. Whereas Kano tried to widen the educational base of the college by inducting talented youngsters, Miura was very much an ex-military (samurai) man and favoured those who were of ex-military stock. He tried to import various aspects of military education into the Gakushuin, such as a cadet system.

Initially the Gakushuin was a private organisation run by the Kazoku-kaikan, but it was not long before it came under the wing of the Imperial Household Agency since the aristocrats were seen as strong supporters of the Imperial family[130]. As a result the Peers School was well funded. All the children of the aristocratic class were required to attend the college regardless of their abilities, however capable non-aristocratic children were allowed in and provided competition for the rest. Kano worked to set up a selection process which separated out the students according to ability. Some of the brightest students were also sent abroad to study. Miura however favoured sending only youths from the military families abroad.

The Gakushuin post lasted for about seven years after which Kano was sent abroad for 16 months by the Imperial Household Agency to investigate education in Europe. See below for more on the Gakushuin and Kano's trip to Europe.

On his return from Europe in 1891 Kano was appointed Head of the No. 5 Upper Middle School (Koto Chugakko) in Kumamoto in Kyushu and Ministry of Education Counsellor. He served in Kumamoto for nearly two years and then in June 1893 he was appointed head of the No 1 Upper Middle school in Tokyo whereupon he returned to Tokyo. Then in a very short space of time he was appointed head of Japan's only male teacher training college (the Tokyo Koto Shihan Gakko) in September 1893, a position which he occupied till 1920 with three short breaks in between. For a while he carried on as head of the No 1 Upper Middle school but eventually had to give it up. As Ministry of Education counsellor he usually had specific tasks within the ministry such as school textbook authorisation, academic system reform or heading the General Affairs section.

At one point he had three jobs on the go, namely Ministry of Education Counsellor, Head of the Tokyo Teacher Training College and Head of the No. 1 Upper Middle School in Tokyo. As can be imagined there was considerable ferment and change in Japanese education as Japan rapidly developed its new education system. See the section on Kano,

---

[130] Following the Meiji Restoration of 1868 court nobles and feudal lords were given the title Kazoku meaning the nobility/peerage. The Kazoku-kaikan means (The Peers Hall).

physical education and the Olympics below for more on the Tokyo Teacher Training College which played a big part in Kano's life.

Apart from the official world of education Kano continued to run his own school, the Kano-juku, for 40 years up to 1922. His Kano-juku covered various educational subjects and judo. Education for Kano was not just poring over books for long hours, but physically experiencing things as well. In 1884, shortly after graduating from Tokyo University, he worked for three years as a lecturer in economics at the Komaba Agricultural University. Kano also ran another school called the Kobunkan from 1882 to 1889 where he engaged former fellow students of Tokyo University to lecture in arts subjects.

Friday Society (*Kinyo-kai*)

Acting as a go-between for Baron Hiranuma Kiichiro (later Prime minister) and Uzawa Somei, Kano helped set up the research group known as the Kinyo-kai (Friday Society) in 1919. Its first meeting was held in the Kazoku-kaikan (the Peers Hall). At the time, Kano was already propagating his views on judo and various social and international problems to his judo students via lectures and in the magazines Judo, Yuko no Katsudo and Sakko (Awakening). The purpose of the Kinyo-kai was to bring together influential and knowledgeable people to exchange views on politics, ideology, economics, education, national defence etc and to talk to the Society. The three originators of the Society called upon their wide contacts to involve first-class representatives from the government, aristocracy, officialdom, the military, education and business. The background to this was the shaky international situation immediately following the First World War, which was also a time of great uncertainty in Japan. This was an attempt to deal with the problems of the time but ultimately it was not able to do anything to stop the drift to the Pacific War.

Kano and physical education and the Olympics

At the same time as Kano was developing his judo, Baron Pierre de Coubertin of France was promoting his Olympic ideal. He started this by expounding the importance of sport at the Paris Exposition of 1889. This coincided with the first of Kano's trips abroad. During this 16 month trip Kano spent his first two months in France, followed by a long spell in

Berlin and finishing with with a quick tour round other European countries. His mission was to investigate education in Europe which he did by visiting colleges and schools and talking to education professionals. It seems very likely that he would have known about the Paris Exposition but there is no evidence of any meeting or correspondence with Coubertin during this time. Possibly his diaries (which he wrote in English) may yield a clue, but these are held by the Kano family. Kano's next trip to Europe was in 1912 which meant that he missed watching the first modern Olympic Games of 1896 and the subsequent 1900, 1904 and 1908 Olympics. (See the section on Kano's trips abroad below)

The first solid reference we have to communication between Coubertin and Kano occurred in the spring of 1909 when the French Ambassador in Japan requested a meeting with Kano. At the meeting he explained that he had received a request from a former college friend, Baron Pierre de Coubertin. The Baron, he said, had organised an International Olympic Committee (IOC) formed of like-minded people, which had already organised four modern Olympic Games in 1896, 1900, 1904 and 1908. The intention thereafter was to continue hosting these Games every four years. The first event consisted of track and field, swimming and a few other sports and the intention was to gradually expand to include more sports. The IOC had delegates from Europe and the United States but none from Asia. The ambassador said he had asked the Japanese Foreign Office and various people in Japan if they could help find a suitable person to represent Japan, providing they and he agreed with the project, and all had recommended him, Jigoro Kano. Would Kano therefore consider this request?

Kano gladly accepted the invitation and became IOC member for Japan and Asia. At the same time he was invited to bring a Japanese team to the next 1912 Olympics. Thereafter Kano attended almost every Olympics and IOC meeting up to his death in 1938, and of course frequently met and corresponded with Baron Coubertin.

Kano was eminently suited for the position as IOC member for Japan. By this time he had been head of the Teacher Training College (Koto Shihan Gakko) for 15 years where he had had a free hand in shaping the college and made physical education an important part of the curriculum. Initially physical education as an academic subject was not highly regarded in Japan – the course was barely a year long – but Kano turned it into a full degree at his college, adding arts and science subjects to the course. His college was the only one to do so in Japan for some time. For example, all his students had to learn to swim, and compulsory long runs and walks were part of the curriculum in addition to four hours a week of exercise or sport of some kind. Kano made newly imported Western sports, Japanese traditional arts such as sumo, kenjitsu and judo and Western sporting competitions a very strong part of the college and PE curriculum. This gave him a lot of publicity – it is said that as many as 20,000 spectators watched some of his college events such as the marathon. Indeed, some of his college competitions (*Dai Undo-kai*) were said to be like mini-Olympics.

Around this time Kano proposed that sumo be included in school physical education as part of a general development of Japanese amateur sport. This led to a lot of amateur sumo activity in Japan, which became the basis for the later establishment of the amateur Japan Sumo Federation (Nihon Sumo Renmei) in 1934. It is said that for quite some time after, amateur sumo was much more popular than the pro-sumo (*Ozumo*) in Japan.

Kano was also founder of the Dai-Nippon Tai-iku Kyokai (Japan Physical Education Association) in 1911. The English title of his new organisation was the Japanese Amateur Athletic Association (possibly copied from the name of the British Amateur Athletic Association). A private body called the Nihon Tai-iku Kai (Japan Physical Education Society) existed already, but was not inclined to support the Olympic ideal despite an offer of help from Kano, so he decided to go ahead with his new association. This Association became necessary when Coubertin suggested to Kano that Japan should set up its own Olympic association to select Japanese athletes to represent the country in the Olympics.

With regard to the naming of this association, some committee members wanted to put the word 'Sport' in the title but Kano refused; threatening to resign and set up another organisation if this was passed. 'Sport' for Kano always meant physical *education* and for a purpose. Kano was rightly called 'the father of Japanese physical education'. The Olympics and his IOC position alone kept Kano very busy.

Unlike Coubertin, Kano was much more involved with the hands-on education of the young. Possibly the Olympic ideal of citius, altius, fortius (swifter, higher, stronger) appealed to his philosophy of self-perfection.

No doubt he would agree with the idea that the most important thing is not to win but take part "not the triumph but the struggle" but I suspect that he would have added the rider; provided you learn from it. Also one suspects he would not be in favour of sport professionalism, drugs, overt nationalism and the win at all costs mentality.

Kano the 'aristocrat' politician

In 1887 Kano was involved in the education of the young future Taisho Emperor at the Gakushuin, where he was both teacher and administrator. Unfortunately the future emperor was somewhat infirm and this became increasingly apparent as he grew older. In 1888 a Privy Council system was put in place and here talented individuals were called on for confidential advice to the emperor. Whether Kano at this point became a Privy Councillor is not known, but certainly his visits to the palace became increasingly more frequent. In 1912 the aging Meiji emperor died and the new Taisho emperor took his place, but he had to rely on a body of advisors and a Regent from 1921 onwards. Up to the point where the Taisho emperor died in 1926 his chief advisors included Prince Saionji Kimmochi and Viscount Katsura, two names which have figured in this book already in close connection with Kano. These were known as *Genro* or Elder Statesmen and effectively controlled Japan for some time.

In 1922, at the age of 62 and having retired from the Tokyo Teacher Training College, Kano was nominated by the Emperor Taisho to become a member of the Japanese House of Peers (Kizoku-in). Kano was not of the aristocracy himself but the system gave the Emperor power to appoint talented individuals to the House. From this point on until his death in 1938, Kano was intimately involved in affairs of state with frequent contacts on both business and personal levels with all the major figures of the government and administration, including the Emperor.

There is one interesting story about his appointment to the House of Peers. Initially Kano was approached privately by an Imperial Household official who, as it happens, was an old student of his. On being informed of the honour he replied somewhat brusquely that he would accept it if it served the country. Kano it seems was not that sure that the appointment would. The student later wrote that if he had not known the character of his teacher well the matter could have terminated there and then.

In addition to the House of Peers there was an elected body known as the House of Representatives (Shugi-in), which was increasingly wracked by political factions and left wing politics[131]. Kano was essentially a supporter of the Imperial family which was not surprising considering his Omi Hiei Taisha Shogenji roots, and therefore against both communists and socialists who were opposed to the Imperial family. For some while the ageing Genro (Elder Statesmen) managed to keep the military and left wing at bay but were eventually unable to stop the army and the navy (controlled by the powerful western Choshu and Satsuma clans) from taking control of the government and shaping the whole course of events which led to Japan's defeat in the Pacific War.

In addition to the prevailing Confucian ideology, Kano seems to have stuck pretty closely to his core beliefs of Seiryoku Saizen Katsuyo, Jita Kyoei and Sojo Sojo, to his support of the Imperial family and to the promotion of education and 'sport'. In so far as he was a counsellor of the Butokukai and the leader of a very large judo organisation he had, in theory, links to the military. This would probably have placed him in a fairly neutral position amid the virulent factional politics of the time.

One wonders quite how he was regarded at the time. Thousands of judo people in Japan were members of the Kodokan and its Black-belt Associations (Yudansha-kai) and could perhaps have been called on by Kano to influence events. His untimely death in 1938, just three years before the outbreak of war in 1941 and the attack on Pearl Harbour, probably deprived Japan of a much needed voice of sanity.

Once Kano became a House of Peers member he travelled very widely and frequently in Japan, often combining his judo interests with his political role. He almost certainly had his finger on the pulse of the nation via his ready-made national organisation of judo-ka, whom he could talk to in confidence, and his many IOC connections abroad. From this time on Kano had many meetings with the Prime Minister, other ministers and senior government officials such as the police. He was also a member of the House of Peers Consultation Committee (Shogi-i-in) which gave him access to the budgetary meetings of key ministries such as the army and navy.

---

[131] The two Houses together comprised the Imperial Diet. This system was changed after the Pacific War.

A clue to Kano's political and other interests can be gleaned from the titles of some of the many talks and lectures he gave in Tokyo and around Japan:

Judo and salvation from the ills of the time (1915)
Basic methods to cure the ills of society (1915)
Fifth Anniversary of Emperor Taisho and what I have to say to my fellow countrymen. (1915)
The Japanese people and judo (1916)
Japanese development abroad (1916)
The power of the individual and the power of society (1919)
Relations between Japan and China (1919)
Perfection of the individual (1922)
The flourishing of the state (1922)
The problem of the leadership of the people (1922)
The prosperity of the Imperial family (1925)
Kodokan judo and the guidance of youth (1926).

A look at just two years in his schedule of engagements shows:

1926
February: Gives a lecture before the Regent Hirohito at the Crown Prince's Palace
March: Attends closing ceremony of the Diet (Parliament)
April: At the request of the Chairman of the House of Peers meets with various House consultation committees
October: Emperor's birthday. Attends banquet at the Imperial Palace
November: Receives a gift from the Emperor of 3000 yen for his Kodokan work
December: Participates in Accession Ceremony of the new emperor Hirohito (after the death of Taisho)

1927
March: House of Peers members (and former students of Kano) throw banquet in Kano's honour
April: Attends the farewell ceremony of the leader of the Privy Council. Attends meeting of the City Government Research

Association. Listens to a speaker's report on the Socialist movement in Japan. Imperial Prince and members of the Diet (Parliament) visit Kodokan to observe judo. Home Office Minister invites senior officials of the provinces to attend talk by Kano

May: Attends secondary education round-table conference. Broadcasts on old-judo and future-judo at Tokyo Broadcasting Centre. Attends Butokukai Festival at the Daikyokuden in Kyoto. Visits Prime Minister to talk to him about the Kodokan Support Group. Visits Elder Statesman Prince Saionji Kimmochi for a chat. Attends Ministry of Education Deliberation Committee meeting on physical education in the prefectures

June: Attends Ministry of Home Affairs (Society Section) meeting

July: Attends Butokukai Competition

September: Attends the military manoeuvers before the Emperor at Fuji Sueno

October: Hears a report on the situation in Asia from the Ministry of Foreign Affairs Asian Section chief. Listens to another report on the Geneva Armament Reduction Conference. Attends the Imperial Review of the fleet at Yokohama

November: Travels to Okinawa to observe karate demonstration.

Kano's political activities and influence on Japan in the 1920s and 1930s would make a very interesting research topic.

Kano's trips abroad

To most Japanese of this time, foreigners and foreign lands were an unknown quantity. Japanese who had even a small amount of social or business contact with foreigners would be very few in number and very few would speak passable English. In an age when most Japanese people had little time, money or the opportunity to travel abroad, Kano went abroad many times either on educational investigations or to attend IOC meetings and events. Many of his trips were quite long. Wherever he went he lost no opportunity to talk about (and demonstrate) judo and emphasise its significance, purpose and educational value. As a result of these early introductions abroad he created many practitioners and lovers of judo in each country, to the point (around 1934) where he thought that the formation of an International Judo Federation was not far off.

Kano's first overseas trip in 1889 was quite a long one, lasting 16 months[132]. It was just before this time that Kano clashed with Viscount Lt. General Miura, the new head of the Gakushuin (Peers College), which led to Kano's resignation. It would seem however that people in high places wanted to retain his services, and made what most Japanese would regard as a tempting suggestion. Kano was asked by the Imperial Household Agency (not the government) to investigate the educational situation in Europe. As already noted two years before this when Kano was working at the Gakushuin he was involved in the education of the future Emperor Taisho[133]. Perhaps the Imperial advisors were interested in seeing what Europe had to offer by way of education (for a future emperor?) or perhaps they simply did not want to lose Kano because of a clash of personalities at the Gakushuin.

Kano arrived in Marseilles and then headed for Paris via Lyon. He spent the first two months of his investigation into education in Paris where he had a lot of contact with the influential French educationalist Ferdinand Buisson and others. Buisson was an academic, pacifist and socialist who helped create the French universal secular primary education system. He later received the Nobel Peace prize in 1927.

It was from about this time that Kano began to think about a new writing system for Japanese. He looked briefly at the predecessor of Esperanto and then came to the conclusion that the best way to write Japanese was not by using the Chinese characters but by using the Western alphabet known as Romaji in Japanese. This interest in Romaji persisted for most of his life. Until quite late on Kano was a member of the Japan-English Language Society (Nichi Eigo-kai) but Romaji never took off in Japan for various technical reasons. Kano returned to Japan in January 1891.

Kano told some amusing stories about his return to Japan by boat from Marseilles. Before going through the Suez Canal he and a small number

---

[132] Kano is generally reckoned to have made nine trips abroad but there are a number of other instances where he travelled to Korea, China and Manchuria which might not have counted as 'abroad' when these territories were part of the Japanese empire. Also when he went to Europe on either educational or Olympic business he sometimes travelled via the Trans-Siberian railway and passed through or stayed in a number of countries.

[133] In Japan the student-teacher relationship can be very strong and last a lifetime.

of passengers decided to get off the boat at Alexandria and go to Cairo to view the pyramids before rejoining the boat further south. They eventually made their way to Cairo and arrived at the exclusive Sheppard's hotel very dusty and travel-stained. This was just in time for the evening meal, but when they had tidied up and gone straight down to the dining room they discovered that all the other guests were wearing evening dress (not that they had brought theirs anyway). Nothing was said but Kano, like most Japanese with a strict attitude to etiquette, would have been keenly aware that they had committed a social faux pas.

The next day they went off to see the pyramids. These were difficult and dangerous to climb but there was no lack of guides to help them – for a price – which jumped remarkably when the climb suddenly got more dangerous. Kano was not prepared to put up with this and climbed up unaided. At the top expensive drinking water was available but Kano refused this also. He explained later that since it was the custom to do judo in Japan during very hot weather without taking water this was no chore for him.

On his second trip abroad in 1902 Kano went to China. In 1896 the Chinese Consul in Tokyo approached Prince Saionji Kimmochi who was then both Foreign and Education Minister to ask if he could recommend a suitable Japanese person to oversee Chinese students studying in Japan[134]. Up to that point the Chinese students had been studying at the Chinese Consulate in Tokyo. China was in some respects in a similar social position to Japan except that Japan had made swifter progress in its modernisation. China had the choice of sending its students to either Europe or America but apparently decided to choose Japan because, as both Chinese and Japanese were written with similar characters, it was fairly easy for the Chinese to learn the language.

Prince Saionji approached Kano who said he had little time but he could possibly recommend and supervise somebody who had more time. Eventually another lecturer at the Gakushuin and former student of Kano – Honda Masujiro – was called upon to direct the education of the Chinese students in a house in Misaki-cho, Kanda ward, Tokyo. Some thirteen Chinese students from the government office of the Chinese

---

[134] Prince Saionji, a calligrapher and scholar, played a pivotal role in Japanese politics and later became Prime Minister.

President qualified through examination and began studying Japanese language, Japanese culture and general education. The school was called *Rakusho-in* [135].

After Japan's success against China in 1894-5 and against Russia in 1904-5 Japan also annexed Korea in 1910 appointing a governor general and imposing colonial rule which lasted to 1945. There then followed an economic and political struggle for influence on the Asian mainland between Japan, Korea and China which eventually led to Japan making the so called Twenty One Demands of 1915, which led to China becoming in effect a vassal state of Japan. This was while Europe was mostly preoccupied with the First World War. Later Russia, Germany and France forced Japan to relinquish its Chinese territories. They were, it appears, all playing the same game but Japan at the time was not strong enough to resist the Europeans.

Kano maintained his supervisory role of the Chinese students and in 1902 was invited to check out the educational situation in China where he toured the country and met top Chinese officials. There was one incident on this trip where Kano was on a small boat and ran into some pirates. During an overnight stand-off he was apparently the only one to keep cool and the incident ended peacefully. Kano, the born educationalist, was keen to help the Chinese with education and he did this for a long time. The Chinese school in Tokyo closed down eventually after politics intruded, and thereafter the Chinese began to send their students to Europe or the USA. Needless to say, while Kano maintained his interest in the school a judo dojo operated there and several of the Chinese students obtained their black belts. Kano was eventually decorated by the Chinese government.

His third trip was to Europe 1912. Unlike his trip to Europe in 1889 when he was ordered to go by the Imperial Household Agency this time he was appointed by the government to investigate education in Europe and America. First he went to Stockholm to attend the fifth Olympic Games and then carried on with his educational mission returning to Japan in 1913. On this trip to Stockholm Kano took with him two competitors, Mishima and Kanekuri. The first was a student from Tokyo Imperial University and the second was a student from his Tokyo

---

[135] Other accounts say it was called Kobungaku-in.

Teacher Training College. He also represented Japan for the first time as its first International Olympic Committee delegate. During these Games Kano was decorated by the King of Sweden (In 1916 there were no Olympic Games because of the outbreak of the First World War in Europe.)

Kano's fourth trip to Europe in 1920 was to attend the sixth Olympic Games in Antwerp. This time he took with him 22 Japanese competitors and led the delegation. After that he toured Europe investigating education in post-First World War Europe.

In September of 1923 the Kanto Great Earthquake occurred. Half of Tokyo and other major cities were razed to the ground, with a loss of life exceeding 100,000. Fortunately this did not affect Kano his dojo or his family. The 7th Olympics was held in Paris in1924. In January 1925 Kano visited London and watched a judo competition at the Stadium Club hosted by the London Budokai led by Tani and Koizumi. (See Chapter 14 on judo's expansion abroad). About this time an attempt was made to create a Far East Olympiad and a few games were held, but Kano appears to have been lukewarm about the idea which eventually faded away.

His fifth trip was in 1928 when he attended an IOC Delegates Conference and the eighth Olympic Games in Amsterdam. He was also the Japanese representative at a world trade conference (Bankoku Giin Shoji Kaigi) and the Inter-Parliamentary Union (IPU) Conference which were on about the same time. He departed from Tokyo station in June, travelled through Siberia by train and arrived in Amsterdam for the Games. Having completed his educational investigations he returned to Japan in September. His attendance as a delegate at the world trade and IPU conferences added an extra political dimension to this trip.

Kano's sixth trip was to attend the tenth Olympic Games in Los Angeles in July 1932. He was accompanied by Takuri, 6th Dan. They toured the North American pacific coast and Hawaii, visiting various cities to introduce and demonstrate judo and encourage the setting up of black belt associations among the many Japanese who settled there. They returned to Japan in September.

His seventh trip in 1933 was to Vienna for the purpose of obtaining an IOC invitation to host the twelfth Olympic Games in Japan in 1940, attending another IPU conference, looking at circumstances in the various

European countries and promoting judo overseas[136]. On this trip he was accompanied by Kotani and Ozaki (both 6th Dans at the time). In 1933 Kano also visited Frankfurt and London where he taught the theory and practice of judo.

His eighth trip in 1934 lasted for five months (April–September) and was for the purpose of attending the IOC conference as Japanese delegate and thereafter touring the chief European countries. On his return he expressed regret that he had been unable to form a world judo federation despite the fact that negotiations had progressed somewhat among the Europeans. 'From that point,' he said, 'discussions would have to proceed by mail or wait for another trip.'[137]

Kano's ninth trip was in 1936 to attend the eleventh Olympic Games and IOC Conference in Berlin. In June he set sail for Europe. I would imagine that both this and his next European trip in 1938 were dogged by talk of war. Japan was of course part of the so-called Tokyo-Berlin-Rome Axis, and waiting and watching were the USSR, America, UK, France etc. Young hot-headed junior officers in the Japanese armed forces were all for taking on the US and the UK, and while wiser heads advised that the logistics were against Japan, the hot-heads countered by saying that they would go down fighting and perhaps their superior fighting spirit would prevail anyway.

His tenth and last trip was in 1938 to attend an IOC meeting in Cairo. He first sailed on the Hakone-maru to Singapore where he boarded a plane for Cairo which arrived safely on 11th March. From 12th March he attended the IOC Conference where he obtained the invitation to host the 1940 Olympics in Japan. On March 20th he broadcast news of this acceptance to Japan. He set sail for Japan crossing the Atlantic and then America itself, but on board the Hikawa-maru, on 4th May at 5.33 in the morning, he died of pneumonia. He was 79 years old.

On this last trip Kano secured an agreement for Japan to host the summer and winter Olympic Games in Tokyo and Sapporo in 1940.

---

[136] This does not seem to have been an educational investigation as were his other trips. It seems that it was common for Japanese who returned from trips abroad to make reports to various government agencies. One Japanese judo teacher who taught in the UK in the 1960s mentioned to me reports that he would have make on his return to Japan.
[137] Judo Zasshi, October 1934.

However this was opposed by certain countries in the IOC because of the complicated situation in world politics at the time. (Japan withdrew from the League of Nations in 1933). Finland, the nation that placed second to Japan in the bidding, offered to host the event, but the outbreak of the Second World War in 1939 forced a complete cancellation of the games until 1948 (when it was held in London). It was not until 1964 that the Olympics went to Japan, but there is no doubt that this was helped by Kano's earlier connection with the IOC. Avery Brundage who became IOC president in 1952 knew Kano well from 1912 onwards.

Chapter 14
Judo Spreads its Wings

Judo was born during difficult times, when Japan was forced to emerge from its long isolation from the world at large and to modernise. In contrast to the long two and a half centuries of peace which Japan enjoyed from about 1600, her emergence from isolation was marked by a succession of conflicts culminating in the Pacific War of 1941–45.

The period was an unforgiving one which turned the world upside down, and many millions suffered or died. Judo, however, managed to survive these uncertain times more or less intact and continued to grow. In 1957 the Kodokan opened its new 1000 plus mat dojo in Kasuga-cho in the Bunkyo ward of Tokyo, and 1964 saw judo in the Tokyo Olympic Games for the first time.

Foreign trainees at the Kodokan
According to Kodokan records the earliest foreign (non-Japanese) student of the Kodokan was the Englishman Captain H.M. Hughes who trained there in 1893. Whether he was from the military or the navy is not known. Next were two Americans, John Forbes Perkins and John Wells Farley in 1899. Between 1882 and 1909 56 foreigners joined the Kodokan for training. One of the Englishmen who joined the Kodokan in 1904 was E.J. Harrison, who later went on to write a number of best-selling books on judo and the Japanese martial arts that helped promote them in the West.

Kodokan accounts of judo abroad
[Japanese accounts of judo abroad do not always square with local accounts of judo's early development. The following is largely based on Oimatsu's account in his book *Judo Gojunen*]

The first record of judo abroad was probably in 1889–91 when Kano embarked on his first educational look-see to Europe. It would appear that Kano did little in the way of judo on this trip but there was one

incident which made him famous in Japan. Whilst on the boat home he
was challenged to a friendly bout by a large Russian naval officer and
threw the officer, which greatly surprised him and the other passengers.
The tussle started with the Russian wrapping his two arms around Kano's
shoulders then trying to twist him over to the left and right. Kano bided
his time then slipped in for a half-hip, half-shoulder throw which sent his
opponent flying. In this famous incident he is said to have demonstrated
his mastery by cushioning the Russian's head and preventing him from
cracking his skull on the metal deck. This story made the headlines in
newspapers in Japan where it was portrayed as a match between Japan and
Russia.

The throw was only part of the encounter. The Russian was boasting
about his strength and challenged any two of the passengers to test their
strength against him in pulling the rudder pole. The Russian won easily,
but Kano murmured to another passenger that he could hold him down
so that he could not get up. Another Russian who spoke English heard this
and relayed it to his boastful friend. Things progressed and Kano did
indeed hold down the man. Then the situation was reversed which led to
Kano going underneath and allowing the Russian to pin him. Kano,
however, quickly turned the Russian over. After this demonstration of
judo it is said that relations between all the passengers were very cordial.
Kano made many trips abroad and never missed an opportunity to
demonstrate his judo.

After that there were one or two naval judo contacts abroad. In 1897
one of the Kano-juku students – naval second lieutenant Yuasa Takejiro 3rd
Dan of Port Arthur blockade fame – voyaged to Melbourne in Australia
and while there gave a demonstration of judo. This was well-received and
reported on in the press. As noted before judo was taught in the Japanese
Naval Academy at Etajima from 1888.

The earliest judo/jujitsu club outside Japan

It is not known what the first jujitsu or judo club outside Japan was, but
the earliest *surviving* club is probably the Seattle Judo Club in the US,
which started around 1903. After that is the Cambridge University Jujitsu
Club in the UK, which began in 1906.

There are however early references to some of the jujitsu prize-fighters
(see below) instructing around the turn of the century. Uenishi (aka Raku)

set up the Piccadilly School of Jujitsu in Golden Square in London a few years before 1906 which is when jujitsu-ka Koizumi Gunji first taught there[138]. Jujitsu did not significantly spread among the general population in this early period although both the police and the military showed interest in it.

Jujitsu fighters

About the turn of the century a number of Japanese judo-ka and jujitsu-ka started travelling abroad on their own initiative, and whilst abroad took on many boxers and wrestlers in prize-fight competitions. Just before the Russo-Japanese war of 1904-5 a group of Japanese, including Maeda Mitsuyo, Tani Yukio, Satake Shinshiro, Ono Akitaro and Miyake Taro, travelled to America and then to Europe. After the European tour Maeda, Satake and Miyake took off to America and Mexico, Tani stayed in London and Ono continued travelling around Europe with a Russian wrestling group. By all accounts they all did very well, especially in winning with arm-locks and strangles, probably like the Gracie jujitsu people in the early days of cage fighting. Maeda Mitsuyo is credited with having taught the member of the Gracie family who went on to create Gracie Jujitsu.

Koizumi Gunji first came over to London in 1906 then took off to America for a while and then back to London in 1910 where he settled permanently. Later, in 1920, both he and Tani opened a jujitsu club in London which they named the Budokwai[139]. Tani was originally from the Fusen jujitsu school and Koizumi studied Tenjinshinyo and Akishima style jujitsu. Both later converted to judo when Kano visited London in 1920. Tanabe Mataemon the master of the Fusen-ryu school of jujitsu was one of the jujitsuka who gave the Kodokan a hard time on the ground in some of the early Kodokan-Jujitsu confrontations. Tani was the principal teacher of Trevor Leggett, who was my principal teacher, which puts the author in the Fusen line perhaps!

Aida Hikoichi came over to the UK with Kano in 1920 and taught in the London Budokwai for two and a half years. In 1931 Kawaishi

---

[138] Cf. A Brief History of the Budokwai by Richard Bowen.
[139] Local records indicate that this was in 1918. (Cf The Bowen Archive in Bath University library)

Mikinosuke came to London where he taught in the Nichi-ei (Anglo-Japanese) Club in London along with Cawkell 2nd Dan for a few years. Then in 1935 he went to France where he settled and played a prominent role in French judo. In 1934 Kano and Nagaoka 10th Dan came to London and on the 21st of July Kano set up the short-lived British Kodokan Judo Yudansha-kai.

There is no doubt that these wandering warriors aroused considerable interest in jujitsu, although it is said that these public competitions began to peter out after about ten years from 1902. After the boom many of the jujitsu-ka carried on teaching abroad. Tani was reputed to have made over a quarter of a million pounds taking on all comers during the period 1902 to 1912, which was a considerable sum, even by today's standards.

Yamashita Yoshiaki 10th Dan

One wandering judo-ka was Yamashita Yoshiaki, later 10th Dan, who resigned from the Tokyo Metropolitan Police (Keishicho) in 1903 in order to go to the United States to give a *Budo* education to the son of Hill the railroad magnate. He went with his wife and taught judo for four years to women's groups, Harvard University students, American Naval Academy students, diplomats, and last but not least President Theodore Roosevelt. During that time he took on and beat several famous wrestlers. He returned to Japan in 1907.

Through his efforts Yamashita is widely credited as having increased American trust of the Japanese, especially during the time of the war between Japan and Russia in 1904-5. In 1905 President Roosevelt arranged a meeting between Japanese Plenipotentiary Komura Jutaro and the Russian Prime Minister Sergei Witte in Portsmouth, New Hampshire where a peace treaty was concluded. It is believed Yamashita played an important part in this meeting.

European judo

In Europe, judo also made early starts in Hungary, Germany and France. This was assisted by not only the jujitsu prize-fighters but by Japanese students with judo experience studying medicine and engineering etc in these countries. As already noted Kawaishi after teaching in London settled in France in the 1930s where he greatly influenced French judo. By 1939 Germany was perhaps the strongest judo nation in Europe with 400-500 registered clubs. Probably the first international judo match was between the Frankfurt Judo Club and the London Budokai in 1929. When Kano first went to Germany and met the German judo-ka he was very surprised to find that they were doing a strange mixture of techniques taken from the book *The Complete Kano Jiu-jitsu (Judo)* written by Hancock and Higashi. Kano knew nothing of this book and quickly pointed out that it had nothing to do with him or his Kodokan judo. In fact the introduction to the book makes clear that two thirds of the techniques in it are from senseis Hoshino (Shiten-ryu) and Tsutsumi (Tsutsumi-ryu?)   only the title is misleading.

Judo in North and South America

Judo in America was mostly on the west coast where Japanese immigrants were concentrated, particularly in Seattle, San Francisco and Los Angeles. There were many dojos in these areas. The black belt associations there had the greatest number of black belts outside Japan. In the east, Chicago and New York had thriving judo communities led by Japanese immigrants.

In Central and South America early judo pioneers were Maeda Mitsuyo and Satake Shinshiro 5th Dan. Both were 4th Dan judo graduates of Waseda University. After graduating in 1904, Maeda travelled to the USA with Tomita Tsunejiro who was 6th Dan at the time. Then he separated from Tomita and travelled to Europe with Satake, Tani and others where they toured England, Belgium, and Spain taking on the locals. After that he went to Cuba, then to Mexico in 1909 and then back to Cuba for a second time. Thereafter he went to Brazil which became his permanent base. He became very popular there under the fighting name he adopted when touring in Spain: Conde Koma (Count Koma). Not only was he famous for judo/jujitsu but he was said to be a big landowner who treated the people on his land with respect. In 1941 he died in Brazil whereupon Satake extended his operations to South America settling down in Mexico.

Apart from Kano and his many trips abroad, Koizumi in the UK and Kawaishi in France were very influential in promoting judo outside Japan and both produced many publications in English and French. The US Supreme Air Command (SAC) was also active after the Pacific War importing top Japanese judo instructors to its SAC bases, although judo did not catch on in the US in the same way that karate did from the 1960s on.

Chapter 15
The End of an Era

The funeral of Kano Jigoro

The funeral of Kano was an extremely sad affair but it beautifully illustrates the measure of the man. When the Hikawa-maru ship reached Yokohama on the morning of May the 6th it had to anchor in the roads because of the portentous sullen weather, but eventually it was allowed to dock at 5pm. Waiting on the quay were family members, relatives and four stalwarts of the Kodokan – 10th Dans Nagaoka, Iizuka, Samura and Mifune. In the next two hours they and representatives from all Kano's walks of life came on board to pay their respects. At 7pm the coffin, over which a large Olympic flag was draped, was carried ashore. A funeral procession of eight cars escorted it to Kano's residence in Tokyo. In the neighbourhood of his Otsuka Sakashita-machi residence many flags of mourning hung from the houses. The coffin was carried up to the second floor by four 8th Dans and reverently placed in the study where Kano had worked for the last 30 years. One after another family, friends and colleagues placed white lilies around it. Kano's wife requested a full Shinto funeral.

On May 7th the coffin was transported to the Kodokan where it was laid on the Shihanseki (the Master's Seat) in the great dojo of the Kodokan. Soon the Kodokan and its corridors overflowed with wreathes and flowers from present and former students and from the nation as a whole, including former Prime Minister Prince Saionji and present Prime Minister Prince Konoe. Attending in person was a never-ending stream of judo students up from the provinces and others from all walks of life including His Imperial Highness Prince Tokugawa Iesato. Through the night they solemnly and silently passed before the coffin paying their last respects.

On May 8th the Emperor Hirohito sent his envoy Makino to the Kano residence bearing *heihaku* (silk or paper cuttings offered to the gods) and funeral service materials. At the same time the family were informed that Kano had been granted the First Class Order of the Rising Sun dated May 4th.

The funeral ceremony was held on May 9th in the Great Dojo of the Suidobashi Kodokan. Before the coffin were placed offerings from HIH Prince Nashimoto, former and present Prime Ministers Saionji and Konoe, Imperial Household Minister Matsudaira, Army Minister Sugiyama, Naval Minister Komeuchi, Minister of Education Kito and many others from the government and nation. 200 people attended the main Service and among the tributes were those from the Butokukai President, the President of Tokyo University, the Governor of Tokyo and the current Head of the Kotoshihan-gakko. Thereafter several thousand people silently passed the coffin to say their last farewells.

Kano's interests were many and varied but he managed to negotiate his Kodokan judo through some extremely difficult times over a long period. He led a long and intense life in which judo and education were his main interests. It would seem that the judo side of that was most intense in his younger years and that a combination of the morality of judo and education was what spurred him on in his later years especially with the worsening international situation.

Perhaps *the* dominant influence in his life was his father Jirosaku. Jirosaku was a generous, very active and able man who helped many extended family members through times of difficulty, and as we have seen he readily yielded his position as head of the Kano family which he came to by way of adoption, to the rightful son and heir. The young Kano obviously aspired to emulate his father, hence his early comment about wanting to go to Edo and become famous. When his father died in 1885 during the so-called 1st Kaminiban-cho Era, Kano described it as the greatest event of that era.

It was the experience of bullying that pushed Kano into jujitsu, which he said curbed his excitability and gave him calmness and a determination which served him well over the years. In the records of some of the organisations to which he belonged, such as the Tokyo Teacher Training College, The Peers College (Gakushuin) and the Japan Amateur Athletic Association, there are accounts of this determination where he was ready to resign rather than compromise his principles – which as we have seen in his judo were strong and well thought out. He was a man who fought hard for what he believed in, but ultimately his belief in his judo principles allowed him to defer and compromise when necessary.

Kano the educational bureaucrat, physical educationalist and jujitsu/judo teacher was the right man at the right time. Without him there would have been no judo or anything like it.

Avery Brundage who was IOC president from 1952-1972 recalled how he first met Kano in 1912, and how many a time 'little Kano' startled his colleagues on the IOC by giving demonstrations of his prowess at judo. It was typical of the man that at the age of 78 he probably died of what is nowadays called in Japan *karoshi* or death from overwork. Possibly on his last trip abroad he also experienced a sense of foreboding about the world situation and how that might affect his beloved judo and the Olympics. When he died in 1938, aged 78, he was leading a life that would have completely exhausted a man of half his age. Kano was a truly remarkable old man.

Without his interest in jujitsu and judo he might well have become prime minister of Japan such were his talents, but certainly he is now much more widely known all over the world for his Kodokan judo than the other Japanese politicians of his time.

In December of 1938 Nango Jiro, a high ranking judoka, naval officer and relative was appointed the new head of the Kodokan. After Nango, the son of Kano Jigoro headed the Kodokan, namely Kano Risei and then his grandson Kano Mitsuyuki.

Chapter 16
Wartime Judo

As can be expected the slow inexorable path to war – from the Mukden or Manchurian Incident of 1931 to the Rome–Berlin–Tokyo Axis of 1940 and the opening of the Pacific War in 1941, with the surprise attack on Pearl Harbour – greatly affected judo in Japan, especially since more and more young Japanese troops were sent overseas as the situation intensified.

The internal wartime organisation of Japan was strengthened, which for Kodokan judo meant coming under the control of the Ministry of Health and Welfare (*Kosei-sho*) which was established in 1938, and the Butokukai. The interest of the Ministry of Health and Welfare in judo was because of its duty to improve the health and fitness of the nation. Judo fell under the Budo training section (*Renbu-ka*) which was formed within the Population Bureau of the Ministry in 1941.

The Butokukai on a war footing

In 1939 it was felt that the martial arts in Japan needed to come under a single controlling body and that a reorganised Butokukai should fulfil that role. This was eventually accomplished in 1942. The stated purpose of the reformed Butokukai was to promote Budo (the military Way) and train the nation. Its head office was moved to the Ministry of Health and Welfare in Tokyo with a branch office in the Heian Shrine in Kyoto.

In the reorganisation the martial arts were listed as:

Kendo which included *Naginata* (halberd), *Iai* (sword drawing), *Jojitsu* and *Bojitsu* (stick-fighting), *Shuriken* (throwing darts etc), *Kusarigama* (sickle and chain) and *Sojitsu* (spear)
Judo which included karate and *torinawa* (binding)
Kyudo (archery)
Jukendo (bayonet)
Shageki-jitsu (marksmanship)

The new Butokukai organisation came under the control of a committee chaired by the Prime Minister along with five cabinet ministers from various connected ministries. A judo section was set up to run judo which became a subsumed group under the Butokukai. This was chaired by Kodokan judoka Arai Gensui.

The former Butokukai ranks were changed to *Renshi* (trainee), *Tasshi* (accomplished) and *Hanshi* (master)[140]. The former ten Dan grades were dropped and replaced by fifth to first *To* (meaning class). Thus 1st Dan became *Go-to* (5th Class), 2nd Dan became *Yon-to* (4th class), 3rd Dan became *San-to* (3rd class), 4th Dan became *Ni-to* (2nd class) and 5th Dan and above became *Itto* (1st class). A Kyu system was retained for those who failed to reach the lowest 5th class (*Go-to*). Note how the number of grades was considerably reduced and that these grades were made to follow the Kodokan Kyu system with the grades starting at 5th-To then dropping down to the highest 1st-To.

Hand-to-hand war combat judo

The final part of the reorganisation of the wartime Butokukai is in many ways the most interesting. Methods of bowing, competition rules, refereeing and teaching principles were revised but in the following section headed 'Teaching Principles Relating to Training' judo is almost turned back to its kumi–uchi/jujitsu roots when it was a method of fighting on the battlefield. Possibly this indicates how the Butokukai might have developed jujitsu from the very beginning without the influence of Kano.

Article 1. Judo is based on bare handed combat and always has to be practised with an actual battlefield mentality. In addition it should be taught as a method of facing an armed opponent

Article 2. Basic movements and techniques (including kata) must be taught and learned as quickly as possible to produce results in battle

Article 3. Judo was originally regarded and practised as an individualistic form of training but should now be taught as a form of group training[141]

Article 4. Judo should be practised realistically out of doors, on grass or sand and in any kind of dress

---

[140] Tasshi replaced the former Kyoshi (teacher).

[141] Kano said individuals should perfect themselves but at the same time described Confucian group activity as 'good'.

Article 5. Emphasis should be placed on training youths in outdoor battle techniques

Article 6. Weak persons should be taught appropriate katas and randori

Article 7. Judo including *Goshin no Kata* is to be spread and encouraged among women and children[142].

Article 8. For those of the rank of Renshi and above, striking (*atemi*) techniques are to be used in competition. Students of the other martial arts (aikido, karate-do, torinawa) must always be taught so that their art can be done in free-fighting form[143].

Article 9. Teachers must fulfil their duties and study other martial arts.

As the war worsened the Ministry of Education announced in 1945 that school children should devote some of their time to warlike activities such as grenade throwing, bayonet fighting, kendo and judo etc. With regard to judo it was agreed that the so-called *Hakuheisengi judo* (close quarter fighting military judo) should be implemented[144]. However many of the changes arrived somewhat late in the day and the end of the war terminated all of them. It is interesting to note how judo was changed to meet the circumstances of war. This was judo stripped down to its bare combat (jujitsu) essentials. How these changes would have worked out if the war had not ended we will never know.

---

[142] Goshin no Kata – self-defence kata – probably a Butokukai kata since at that time the Kodokan did not have a Goshin no Kata or Goshinjitsu.

[143] Note how in Article 8 *atemi* was incorporated in free-fighting for Renshi and above.

[144] Not easy to translate. *Hakuhei* means drawn sword, hakuheisen means close quarter fighting with sharp weapons, *sengi* means military technique. The general idea is that this is last resort wartime hand to hand and eyeball–to–eyeball fighting.

Chapter 17
Post-War Judo

Not long after the Allies had dropped two atomic bombs, one on Nagasaki and the other on Hiroshima, Emperor Hirohito took decisive control and announced to the nation in a radio broadcast that the war had ended. Most of the listeners barely understood his ancient court language but his intent was clear. Without a fuss the nation acted as one and surrendered, despite allied fears that they would fight to the last man, woman and child if the foreign invaders stepped on Japanese soil. In August of 1945 Japan agreed to the Potsdam Declaration of the Allied terms for Japan's surrender. The terms included Japan's demobilisation and demilitarisation, the punishment of war criminals and the limitation of Japanese territory to the four main islands of Japan (Honshu, Hokkaido, Shikoku and Kyushu).

The agreement was signed on the 2nd of September 1945. Apart from the fear of further nuclear attacks Japan was also concerned about the threat from the communist Soviet Union, which with the defeat and partition of Germany was now turning its attention to its far eastern territories bordering Japan, and was perhaps considering the partition of Japan as well.

The dissolution of the Butokukai
In post-war Japan the Allied occupiers regarded Japanese ultra-nationalism, militarism and anti-democratism as its three main targets.

The martial arts came under the heading of militarism and were put under the control of the Allies and its Civil Information and Education Section (CIS), headed by Brigadier General Dike. In implementing the terms of the Potsdam Declaration the Japanese were given a certain amount of leeway but the final say was with General MacArthur – the Supreme Commander of the Allied Powers[145]. Two of the first things the

[145] A joke I heard from a number of Japanese in the 1960s was that if you got up early enough you could see McArthur walking on the imperial moat.

CIS did in November 1945 were to ban judo and kendo from the school curriculum and university campuses, and to ban the word Budo. However individuals were allowed to carry on training privately and private institutions such as the Kodokan were also allowed.

As already noted the Butokukai was supposedly a private martial arts umbrella organisation and foundation dating from 1895, but its connections with the police, Imperial family, high-ranking politicians and provincial officials and soldiers made it a de facto state run organisation. Inevitably it attracted the attention of the Allies. There was a short period during which the Butokukai tried to justify its existence and retain what it could of its organisation and powers, but in July 1946 the CIS saw a contradiction between Butokukai activity and the terms of the Potsdam Agreement, which prohibited the continuation of militarism, the spread of warlike spirit and the spread of radical nationalistic concepts in occupied Japan.

There then followed a period of 'negotiation' but the CIS, tiring of this, suspended the Butokukai activities. Thereafter at the first meeting of its directors and then a second meeting of its councillors the Butokukai was formally dissolved on October 31st 1946.

Along with the banning of judo and kendo the term Budo was banned from the school curriculum and from university campuses from November 1945 onwards, and teachers of these arts lost their licence to teach. In addition Budo equipment was not allowed to be stored on school premises and dojos had to be changed to other use (This ban lasted till October 1950.)

The democratisation of Japanese judo

After the Pacific War the Allies also felt some dissatisfaction with the Yudansha-kai (Dan grade Associations) which controlled many areas of Japanese judo. The need was felt to create democratic and autonomous bodies which would include both black belts and non-black belts. At the same time, world and continental groupings were swiftly emerging, such as the International Judo Federation and the European Judo Union. This posed the awkward question of who would represent Japan internationally. Would it be the Kodokan or a new Japanese judo federation? The answer was clear and the All Japan Judo Federation (Zen Nihon Judo Renmei) was born in 1949 but with Kano Risei (son of Kano Jigoro) as its president. Thereafter the Kodokan and the All Japan Judo Federation were like two sides of the same coin – a typical Japanese compromise.

In 1950 judo was allowed back into Japanese schools as a compulsory subject along with kendo. The Kodokan continued as a grade-awarding body and many of its top men occupied key positions in the All Japan Judo Federation. The HQ of the Japanese Judo Federation was also located in the Kodokan building in Kasuga-cho as was the International Judo Federation when Kano Risei was its first President.

In 1950 the Korean War began. The ending of the American occupation of Japan followed in 1952. Japan was no longer regarded as the enemy of America but an ally. As with Judo's early history war yet again played its part in judo development.

The internationalisation of Japanese judo

The first judo world championship in Tokyo in 1956 was followed by judo's inclusion in the 1964 Tokyo Olympic Games. At this point judo came of age as an international sport – but probably not quite as Jigoro Kano had envisaged. Japan, with its long experience of judo, saw itself as the leader of judo's international development and strenuously resisted many of the post-war innovations such as weight categories, small scores (*koka* etc), passivity warnings and blue judo suits. However such was the democratic nature of the IJF that these measures were voted through and Japan had a choice of living with the changes or opting out altogether. Judo's inclusion in the Olympic Games effectively prevented that. Kano Jigoro was after all Japan's first IOC member.

On the political front, national, continental and world organisations quickly consolidated. For example, just before the formation of the British Judo Association, British judo was loosely run by the London based Budokai with its 80 or so affiliated clubs. Once the BJA was formed in 1948 the Budokai terminated its affiliated club system and during the period 1945-1965 the BJA grew to more than 1000 clubs which well illustrates the phenomenal growth of world judo during this period. Up to this time judo was just about the only oriental martial art around, and until other competitors such as karate and kung fu arrived on the scene it flourished everywhere. As can be expected the inclusion of judo in the Olympics gave it a huge boost, as countries which hitherto had not done judo began training for the Olympics.

Up to about 1948 judo was done because it was regarded as an effective form of self-defence, for its physical training and character enhancing benefits and because the black belt system gave students a worthwhile goal. From about 1960 onwards international competition spread rapidly and competitors began to focus less on the belt worn around their middle than on the medals they could win in competition. The grading system became less of an attraction. However, most judoka wanted to wear a black belt and stayed in the grading system to 1st Dan. Since there was nothing to differentiate a 1st Dan from a 5th Dan many terminated their grading efforts at 1st Dan. When the Soviet Union first began participating in international judo competitions many of its competitors came on to the mat wearing belts of varying colours (apparantly Soviet judo did not believe in grades – all its participants were simply sportsmen). They were then told that according to the rules the minimum grade for competition was black belt. So a Soviet official was despatched to buy a box of black belts which the competitors then wrapped around their middles before they came out to fight. Despite various attempts to create an international grading system nothing emerged except for a brief period when Dr. Matsumae was IJF president. National organisations began running their own systems most of which were loosely based on the Kodokan and British ones.

The first President of the International Judo Federation which was founded in 1950 was Kano Risei, the son of Kano Jigoro. No-one in the Japanese judo world (or anyone else for that matter) had much experience of running a democratic international judo organisation, and after some criticism of the way Japan liased with the rest of the IJF members, some political in-fighting resulted in the Englishman Charles Palmer becoming president of the IJF in 1965 by default, and holding the position for 14 years. Palmer was eventually replaced by Matsumae Shigeyoshi of Japan who ran the Tokai educational organisation. This provoked a certain amount of Japanese political in-fighting which spilled abroad. Eventually Matsumae was replaced by the South Korean Kim, who reigned till 2007 when a Romanian by the name of Marius Vizer was elected.

Judo as sport

Kano died in 1938 when sport was carried out by either strict amateurs or professionals. The professionals were those who took money for sport either as coaches or in prize money and they were not allowed to compete in championships such as the Olympic Games which were strictly for amateurs. Kano was a child of his time and did not dispute this distinction. Indeed his attitude to judo and money was quite strict. For example he did not think that people should pay for judo instruction and charged nothing for it in the Kodokan. However, Kano was not able to forsee the growth of modern competitive sport and its links with state sponsored sport for nationalistic ends and the influence of television. He was however in a unique position to forsee immediate future trends especially because of his headship of the Tokyo Teacher Training College with its strong physical education department and its promotion of many Western 'competitive exercises'. As already noted his college marathons attracted huge crowds and publicity.

The debate about judo as sport or judo as martial art raged in Japan and still does to a degree there and elsewhere. Kano wrote on the subject in the magazine Sakko in 1929 under the title *Judo to Kyogi Undo*[146] (Judo and Competitive Exercise). What follows is an abstract of that article:

'In recent years as competitive exercise has become more popular questions have often arisen about the relationship of judo to it. The form of the questions differ but on one extreme are those who say we should reject imported competitive exercise judo since we have our own unique martial arts which are good for physical and mental education. They go on to say that if we practise our own martial arts the Japanese spirit will be cultivated but if we get addicted to the foreign competitive exercises we will become like foreigners in our souls. On the other hand there are those who advocate the advantages of imported competitive exercise saying we should democratise judo in training and competition.

In both cases these miss the point. It is very necessary to make clear the original relationship between the two extreme points of view. In the first place the judo I advocate at all times in every way is a broad church. It divides into different compartments depending on its types of application − such as a martial art, physical education, intellectual and moral education or as a way of leading one's real life (*jisseikatsu*).

---

[146] Cf the second volume of Kano Jigoro Chosakushu pages 376 to 380.

However competitive exercise is a type of exercise which naturally trains the body and the spirit. One cannot dispute the fact that if the methods of competitive exercise are relied on they will have a big effect on physical and mental training.

Nevertheless, the objectives of competitive exercise are simple and narrow but the purpose of judo is complicated and wide. In other words competitive exercise only achieves one portion of judo's objectives. Of course judo can be treated competitively, which is good, but if that is all that is done the original purpose of judo cannot be achieved. For that reason while agreeing that judo as a competitive exercise meets the spirit of the time we must never forget where judo's real character lies. The real character of judo is sternly evident and even if one treats judo as a competitive exercise which meets the spirit of the times there is scope to debate the wrongs and rights of this. Even if judo does meet the spirit of the times if it does not have a basic reason for doing so it may be necessary to oppose it.

A closer examination of the basic problem cannot be regarded today as a useless task. It is already clear that it is unreliable to treat judo as the same as other competitive exercises now carried on in the outside world. The argument that judo is a struggle for victory and that it cannot be carried out competitively does not hold water.

When it comes to the question whether to exhibit this competition to the public and to make it widely understandable to the people or to keep it privately in a dojo as in former times I think that showing it competitively is a good strategy for breaking these old private customs. I think that nobody would dispute this.

However the next problem is whether it is appropriate to show it to the public like any other competitive exercise and charge an entrance fee. This problem has been under consideration for quite some time and my thoughts on the matter are decided but I have been cautious because our country's customs have existed for a long time and I have thought to adopt the principle gradually.

The reason why this country has not been pleased to run competitions and charge for spectator entry was because of the bad name that geinin (artistes, entertainers and performers) had acquired by charging an entry fee. This was because of the rowdy behaviour they exhibited to their listeners, spectators, stewards and patrons. So when the phrase 'entrance fee' is heard nowadays people take it the wrong way and do not regard it as artistic performance.

In Europe and America matters are otherwise. Public performances are attended by royalty, aristocrats, gentlemen and students in purpose built buildings and do so not for personal benefit but for public benefit and out of interest.

This is like the three Olympic Games that I have attended. These had royalty as patrons. Whichever country hosts these games money is required for building the facilities. Presently in Japan the Meiji Shrine Athletic Tournament has Princess Chichibu as a president. The participants are gentlemen and students and the event has a certain refinement. I doubt that the sponsors would be able to raise sufficient money if an entrance fee was not levied. The state has limited money and cannot support everything.

I think it is acceptable to rely in part on donations and state aid but generally speaking I think it best that such events are supported by lovers of the sport and its technique if they are held for the development and vigorous growth of the game.

It is very necessary not confuse an athlete with a performer. In the Stockholm Olympics of 1912 one athlete won his event and received prize money from somebody. He was not a professional but it seems that he had received many prizes in the past in his own country. It caused a stir and the prize money had to be handed back as I recall. On my way home to Japan I went to America and met President Taft. After asking me if I was on my way back from the Olympics he said that he had heard an American athlete had done a regrettable thing. I understood from the conversation that he disliked such a commercial action and valued amateur athletics.

For this reason I have no objection to charging entrance fees provided the use of such fees is beneficial and transparent. Rather I regard it as necessary for the times we live in.

From the above I believe that the question of the relationship between judo and competitive exercise can be solved. The Kodokan should proceed in future on this principle. This is not to say that the Kodokan will never invest in competitive facilities and actions. There will not be the slightest deviation from the essential character of the Kodokan and its original principles. When judo is being treated competitively I see no necessity to distinguish it from other sports.

Today the average student plays judo in this competitive form. If that is bad judo should not imitate it and it should be stopped. Students do other types of competitive exercise competitively which is fine. It is no excuse to say that that is only bad when doing judo. I approve of the competitive exercise that we do now if it is done as exercises by gentlemanly amateurs. I do not agree with the quibble that judo should not join their company.'

So Kano it seems was not opposed to public competitions of judo which started to grow rapidly from about 1900 onwards provided that the contestants did not 'perform' or receive prize money. Many of the earlier competitions such as the All-Japan Judo Championships were fought in specialist (teachers) and non-specialist divisions but not for prize money in the case of the specialists. That also happened in the European Judo Championships around 1965. He was however keen to avoid the type of rowdy public performances that sometimes happened in Japan in other arts such as sumo. In so far as judo training is mainly randori which is very competitive it is hardly logical to say that it should not be done in competitive form like other (Western) sports. Perhaps Kano would not have liked the growth of the many competitors who compete endlessly for trophies or medals. Somehow the competition venue or the training camp has become the main place for training not the dojo.

A gap is growing between the dojo judoka and the competitors. This is shown in the competition rules which do not fully apply to the dojo training (such as passivity penalties) and the wearing of the blue suit in the dojo. In most countries competitors are numerically quite few. In the UK for example competitors only account for about 5–10% of the judo membership. So judo is being changed and led by the minority – the competitors. Competition judo and dojo judo should be kept the same as possible and that way perhaps the three objectives of judo can be pursued.

# Postscript

Predictions

In one of my lectures at Bath University I was asked to make some predictions about judo, which I know is a risky business. As the Japanese saying goes, 'just one inch into the future is complete darkness' (*Issun saki wa yami*).

If I had to give a potted history of world judo to the present I would say that it first emerged from jujitsu which developed during a very long period of peace in Japan. Then for the first 60 years of its existence as judo it developed very slowly indeed except in Japan where four major wars hastened its growth. After the Second World War judo grew very rapidly outside Japan, especially in the period 1945-1965. Why this should be so is not clear. One would have thought that the soldiers who returned from the war would have had enough of fighting or perhaps they were impressed with the fighting skills of the Japanese soldiers they fought. However judo was the first martial art of the post-war scene to arrive in the West and had a monopoly for some time. In the 1960s other martial arts such as karate, taekwondo and kung fu arrived and challenged judo's monopoly.

Judo, however, was greatly stimulated by being included in the 1964 Olympics and has continued to grow on the back of the Olympics. This growth is shown more in the number of countries doing it than in any general increase per country. If it had not become an Olympic sport I would hazard a guess that judo might have wilted under the rivalry of other oriental martial arts. Currently judo is somewhat dependent on its Olympic status which is by no means assured. Many other sports seek to enter the Olympics and the International Olympic Committee is constantly seeking ways to trim its evergrowing programme.

Judo therefore cannot afford to rest on its laurels. It has to make sure that its competition rules are logical, well written and understood by the public (which currently they are not). It has to ensure that it is regarded as an effective martial art and it must allow longer on the ground for submission techniques. In addition it needs to combine the foregoing with a determined drive to foster spectacular high throws. Every judoka knows that it is the big throw that excites the crowd, and yet nobody seems to use the rules to stimulate such spectacular action. Writing in height as one of the necessary Ippon throw criteria might achieve that.

In my Bath lectures I listed three influences on judo. They were conservatism, realism and 'sportification'.

Conservatism seeks to keep judo as it was first created and of course the arch-conservatives are the Japanese and those judoka who look to Japan for leadership. However, when it comes to blocking any IJF proposal that might change judo for the worse (in their eyes), Japan only has one vote. By and large judo has not changed that much and the Japanese have adapted reluctantly to the changes.

One possible scenario is that if changes went too far the Japanese conservatives could always opt out of the Olympics etc and set up their own world organisation, which could seriously dent the IJF as many countries might decide to go along with it. Judo continues to change slowly and the question is, how far will the Japanese go along with this? Japanese judo has a moral dimension to it and if this was threatened in any major way Japan might feel it had to go it alone. Note that despite the growth of judo outside Japan it continues to head the gold medal table in major competitions.

Realism is another slowly creeping influence and this is most strongly evident in the concept of judo as a combat art. In the judo boom times of 1945-65 judo was perhaps naively regarded as the ultimate combat sport. It was advertised as the method by which a weaker smaller man could overcome a stronger man by using his strength against him. Then along came the more spectacular karate, kung fu and kick-boxing and people were not quite so sure about judo. Whereas fight scenes in many early movies showed fisticuffs or occasional judo moves this rapidly changed when the other martial arts arrived. Some time later when cage fighting (UFC) appeared on the scene the grappling arts (judo, Gracie jujitsu, wrestling etc) beat the striking arts (karate, kick-boxing, Taekwondo etc) with their armlocks, strangles and some striking techniques. Many judo people just nodded and said 'We told you so', but that did not necessarily increase the numbers coming into judo. Mostly

Gracie (Brazilian) jujitsu benefitted from this which in reality consisted largely of judo techniques.

Although Kano made a convincing case for limiting access to groundwork by stating that in a fight against more than one assailant it was better to stay on one's feet, the contest rules were never really directed towards that. Judo people continue to fall over when making throws. Now, with increased restriction of groundwork the pendulum has swung too far so that very few bouts are won with submission or restraint techniques. These are the very techniques that the early Japanese jujitsu-ka and later the cage fighters used to beat the boxers.

It is assumed that people do judo for rational reasons and its potential as a combat sport must be one of them. However that is not to say that people do judo for self-defence reasons. Somebody who has been mugged might feel the need to join a judo class but in my experience very few judoka want to work on self-defence in the dojo. What people want to do is something which would be useful in an extreme situation. Judo's hard physical training and the ability to throw, strangle, lock and restrain assailants fulfil this but it must be careful not to drift into the symbolism of Olympic wrestling. Judo has to be careful to preserve its combat credentials; otherwise the numbers might begin to decrease at a grass roots level.

Present day Olympic wrestling faces similar challenges but it changes its rules with far greater frequency than judo, which moves very slowly in this respect. Recent 2005 wrestling rule changes have brought in scoring for throws. Wrestling has also recently included what it calls 'grappling' under its wrestling umbrella (FILA). Grappling is wrestling which includes submission holds (locks and strangles). This may or may not take off but it is clearly a move into judo territory. This needs to be carefully monitored.

'Sportification', the last of my trio of influences, is the pressure on judo to follow other successful sports as seen on television. Some of this is driven by new technology, such as video-recall for the referees and judges and instantaneous electronic scoring (which have to be a good thing), and introducing more razzamatazz and colour, which of course starts to approach the nonsense of pro-wrestling. If done it has to be done carefully.

The competition rules also need to be carefully re-written by a legislator-judoka-lawyer. These rules ultimately shape judo but are presently in a bit of a mess. One clear influence to be seen at present is the incursion of wrestling moves into judo, such as leg-takedowns, fireman's lift and the 'flop and drop' style of throwing. These look messy and unspectacular. The rules need to concentrate on making judo spectacular again and establishing its distinctiveness – its USP or unique selling points.

Perhaps the wisest course is to stick to the *three* objectives of judo as laid down by Kano Jigoro, giving each equal consideration. We must be careful that judo does not slowly slide away from us. If it does it will be imperceptibly, such as by slow decline in people starting judo. The judo federations need to watch their membership numbers.

One wonders what Kano would make of judo nowadays. Technically he would note that there is not much groundwork, that judo is fought in weight categories and that there are not that many clean throws. Visually he would note the coloured mat area and the blue judogi and he would see many adverts in response to the financial demands of televison. If he were to talk to coaches at a major championship he might discover that there was very little emphasis on judo's original character-training objective or its combat objective, and that most of the competitors do judo because it is a 'sport' which provides them with a certain amount of fame and fortune – though nowhere near as much as other major sports.

However if he were to visit modern dojos he would find them full of people who gain immense satisfaction and many benefits from judo training and the ethos of judo. Judo administrators and politicians must be very careful to retain what is good about judo and not try to fix something that is not broke. The sport of judo must not be allowed to override the culture of judo.

Bibliography

- *Judo Kyohon* by Kano Jigoro. Sanseido, 1931
- *Judo Gojunen* (fifty years of judo) by Oimatsu Shinichi. Jiji Tsushinsha, 1955
- *Dai-Nippon Judo-shi* (A History of Japanese Judo), edited by Maruyama Sanzo. Kodokan in 1939
- *Kano Jigoro* (biography). Kodokan, 1964
- *Kano-Sensei-den* (tales of Professor Kano) by Yokoyama Kendo, Kodokan, 1941
- *Kano Jigoro Chosakushu* (writings of Jigoro Kano). 3 Vols. Gogatsu Shobo, 1983

- *Judo Kyohan* by Yokoyama and Oshima, Nishodo 1924
- *Nippon Budo Zenshu*. Vols 1-6. (Japanese Budo/bujitsu). Jinbutsu Orai-sha, 1966
- *Jujitsu Nyumon* (jujitsu for beginners) by Kanno Hisashi, Airyudo, 1989
- *Jujitsu Kyohan* (Jujitsu teacher) by Anegawa Shogi. Airyudo, 1963
- *Kashima Shin-ryu* (Kashima Shin martial arts school) by Seki Fumitake. Kyorin Shoin, 1976
- *Judo Zasshi* - the Kodokan monthly magazine.
- *Kendo Hikkei* (Kendo companion) by Hiromitsu Hidekuni. Kendo Shimbun-sha, 1971
- *Sumo no Rekishi* (sumo history) by Nitta Ichiro. Yamakawa, 1994
- *Sumo Shijuhatte* – the 48 techniques of Sumo – by Kasagiyama & Hiresaki. Baseball Magazine-sha, 1986
- *Historical Grammar of Japanese* by Sansom. Oxford University Press, 1928
- *Kodokan Judo Kagaku Kenkyukai Kiyo* (Kodokan Judo Science Bulletins), 1958-84 (Vols 1-6)
- *Judo Shiai Shimpan Kitei* (Judo Competition Rules) by Morishita & Murayama. Gakugei, 1973
- *Judo Koza* (Judo Lectures). Vols 1-3 by Mifune, Kudo, Matsumoto. Shiramizu-sha, 1956
- *Judo no Kenkyu* (A study of Judo) by Hayashi Kunitaro. Chugai Noki-sha, 1925
- *Chugoku Bujitsu* (Chinese Martial Arts) by Matsuda Masashi. Shinjinbutsu Orai-sha, 1972
- *Japanese History* by Sansom & others.
- *Zen and the Ways* by Trevor Leggett. RKP, 1978

Appendix 1: The Kodokan Dojos

Dojo[147]	Dates	Period	Mat size
Eisho-ji	Feb 1882 to Feb 1883	=1 year	8 mats
Kobunkan	Feb 1883 to Sep 1883	=6 months	10 mats
Kami Niban-cho (1)	Sep 1883 to Mar 1886	=2½ years	20 mats
Fujimi-cho	Mar 1886 to Apr 1889	=3 years	40 mats

[147] NB. Old dojos were not always closed down but sometimes used for different purposes such as schools.

Dojo	Dates	Period	Mat size
Masago-cho	Apr 1889 to Apr 1891	=2 years	70 mats
Kami Niban-cho (2)	1891 to 1893	=2 years	20 mats
Shita-tomizaka-cho[148]	1893 to 1906	=13 years	100 mats
Shita-tomizaka dojo	1906 to 1933	=27 years	300 mats
Suidobashi	1933 to 1958	=25 years	510 + mats
Bunkyo-Kasuga-cho	1958 to date	=50 years	1000+ mats

Appendix 2: Japanese names and pronunciation

In Japanese personal names the family name comes first, so the founder of judo is Kano Jigoro. I follow this order with other Japanese names in the book. In Japanese books Kano is mostly referred to as the Shihan meaning the Master. Since there are very many references in this book to him I have mostly referred to him as Kano. No disrespect is intended.

Although there are different ways of doing it a Japanese noun is not usually changed to make it plural. For example dojo can mean one or more than one dojo. Usually it is clear from the context what is meant. However, when using common Japanese words in English the tendency is to add an 's' as in *dojos*. The alternative is to say 'I worked out in two dojo' which sounds clumsy.

For the purposes of this book, the following is a simple explanation of pronunciation (in practice it is a bit more complicated than this):

Vowels in Japanese can be long or short and it is important to get them right, or you will not be understood. When writing a Japanese word in English the long vowel is often distinguished by writing a line over it. For example judo should be written jūdō. Sumō is pronounced with a short 'u' and a long 'o' which makes it sound like 'smo' (to rhyme with snow). However, most non-Japanese do not pay much attention to this so I have not followed the practice. In the Glossary I indicate the correct vowel pronunciation for the most common words. Throughout the book I do not.

Japanese vowels are nearly always pronounced the same, unlike English:

'a' is pronounced as in 'car'
'i' is pronounced as in 'kit'

---

[148] Some functions of the Shita-tomizaka-cho dojo transferred to Otsuka-sakashita-machi which was named the Kaiunzaka dojo. In 1933 the Kaiunzaka dojo functions moved into the new Suidobashi dojo.

'u' is pronounced as in 'cool'

'e' is pronounced as in 'pet'

'o' is pronounced as in 'cot' or 'coat'

'y' is pronounced as 'i' above. (The 'y' in '*ryo*' or '*gyaku*', is pronounced 'rio' and 'giaku', and never like the 'y' in 'why')

Two or more vowels together are pronounced separately: 'ie' is 'i-e'. Consonants are much the same as in English except 'g' is hard as in 'good'. Two consonants together are pronounced separately. *Hikkomi* is 'hik-komi' but said quickly.

'Ts' as in *tsurikomi* is pronounced like the end sound of pits.

Some consonants are interchangeable such as g & k, h & b and sh & j with no change of meaning. For example katame and gatame, harai-goshi and ashi-barai, shime-waza and juji-jime.

Common mistakes are to pronounce 'i' for 'e' at the end of words. Ie gatami instead of gatame. *Hantei* is pronounced 'han-tay'. *Newaza* is pronounced 'neh-waza' not 'knee-waza'.

Glossary

Atemi	Striking techniques
Bunbu no Michi	The Way of the Pen and the Sword
Bunbu Ryōdō	The dual path of the Pen and the Sword
Daimyō	Feudal lord
Dan	Advanced grade
Gi	Judo suit
Gō	Hard, resistant
Gokyō	The Five Teachings (40 throws)
Goshinjitsu	Self-defence Sequence
Han or Ban	Feudal domain
Ippon	Winning Technique
Itsutsu no Kata	The Kata of Five Movements
Jitakyōei	Mutual Welfare and Benefit
Jū	Soft, yielding, compliant
Jūdō-gi	Judo costume. Often called *gi*.
Jūdō-ka	Judo practitioner
Jūjitsu	Unarmed (or lightly armed) Japanese combat systems

Jū no Kata	The Kata of Ju
-ka	Suffix meaning 'practitioner of'
Kangeiko	Mid-winter Special Training
Kata	Pre-arranged technique sequences/drills
Katame no Kata	The Kata of Groundwork
Kime no Kata	The Kata of Decisive Techniques
Kōhakushiai	Red and White Contests
Koshiki no Kata	The Kata of Ancient Forms
Kuzushi	Balance breaking
Kyū	Beginner grade
Kyūba no Michi	The Way of the Bow and Horse
Kyūsho	Vital nerve spot
Maitta/Mairi!	I give in/submit!
Nage no Kata	The Kata of Throws
Ne-waza	Groundwork
Randori	Free-fighting, sparring
Rei	Etiquette, bow
Roku Bugei	The Six Martial Arts
Seiryoku Saizen Katsuyō	Highest practical application of mind and body
Seiryoku Zenyō	Moral use of Mind and Body
Seiryoku Zenyō- Kokumin Tai-iku	The People's Physical Education (based on the principle of Seiryoku Zenyo)
Shiai	Contest
Shōbu	Another word for *shiai*
Shōbu-hō	Combat objective of judo
Shochūgeiko	Mid-summer Special Training
Shōgun	Military ruler
Shugyō	Ascetic training
Shūshin-hō	Moral objective of judo
Sōjo-sōjō	Mutual aid and deference
Sutemi-waza	Sacrifice throws
Tachi-waza	Standing techniques
Tai-iku-hō	The physical education objective of judo
Waza-ari	A near-full score, equivalent to 70% of full one
Yukō no Katsudō	Effective practical application
Zen	Buddhist meditational sect

Index

FURTHER ORDERS

For further orders go to **www.sydhoare.com**.